COMPLETE GUIDE TO PYTHON TURTLE

PYTHON TURTLE

P.KARTHICK CHANDRU

First i thanks to my parents

And i dedicated this book to whom buy my book ....

Contents

Foreword

Hello guy`s first of all thank you for reading my book in this book i tell about how to learn python turtle this book more suitable for who are all intersetd in coding and also it is useful for who are all beginners in i python turtle telled step by step method to do graphics in python turtle. lets get started.............

"COMPLETE GUIDE TO PYTHON TURTLE" Author: P.KARTHICKCHANDRU (2021)

Preface

Hello guy`s Thank you for reading my book and you can dedicate this book to your friend who are most intrested in python turtle. first of all why i choosed to write about this topic because I more intersted in computer language like python,c++and so on..... why I more interseted in computer language there was a story behind that when i was 11 years old I played more video games sometimes its very bored to me. one day I think that why can we make games so, I start to learn pythonwhen I was 12 years old and my inspiration and role model was myself...

Acknowledgements

I would like to express my special thanks of gratitude to my parents as well as my friends who gave me the golden opportunity to write this wonderfull book on the topic complete guid to python turtle, which also helped me in doing a lot of research and i came to know about so many new things iam really thankful to them.

CHAPTER ONE

LEARN PYTHON TURTLE

1.History of logo and turtle graphics :

** In 1967, Seymour Papert and Wally Feurzeig created an interpretive programming language called Logo.*

** Papert added commands to Logo so that he could control a turtle robot, which drew shaped on paper, from his computer.*

** Turtle graphics is now part of Python.*

** Using the Turtle involves instructing the turtle to move on the screen and draw lines to create the desired shape.*

2.Basic turtle command:

There are four basic turtle commands:

forward(x)

Moves turtle forward in direction it is facing by x steps

back(x)

Moves turtle backward from its facing direction by x ste

left(x)

Turns the turtle x degrees counterclockwise

right(x)

Turns the turtle x degrees clockwise

3.Turtle Modules:

Turtle is a Python module. It's an extra part of the Python

language, so we need to import its functions by turtle

putting an statement at the top of each program.

*from turtle import **

forward(100)

*type the above code in python shell The * means everything,*

so this imports all of the functions from the module.

Run this example to turtle see what it does!

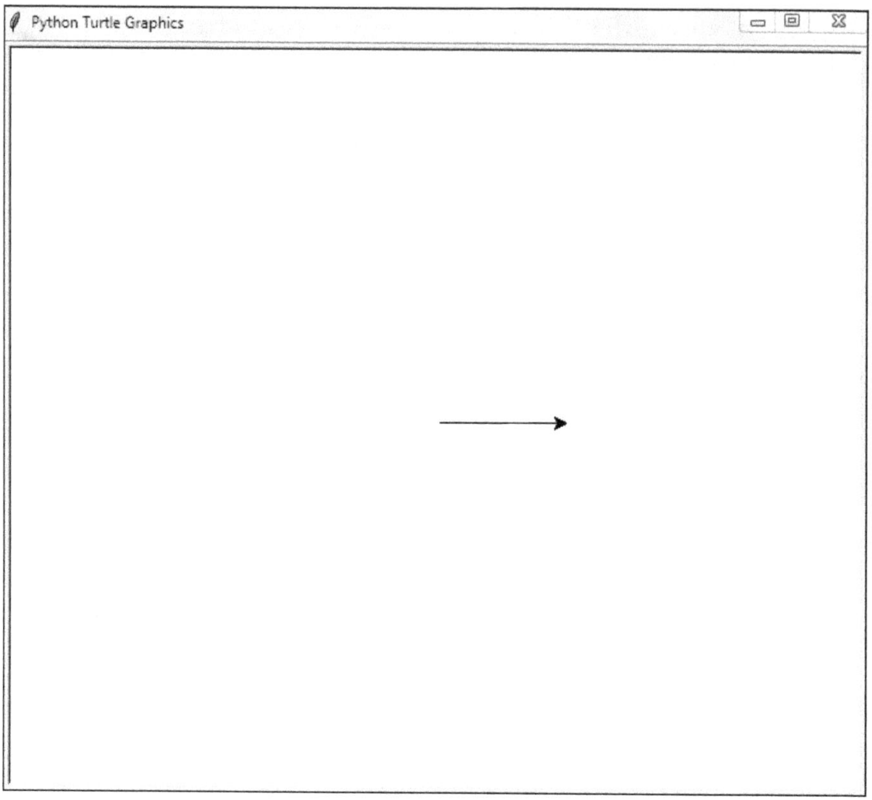

python turtle graphics

4.How to submit the program:

Write your program (in the file) in the editor program.py

(large panel on the right);

2. Run your program by clicking Run .

The turtle will appear below.

Check the program works correctly!

3. Mark your program by clicking

Mark and we will automacally check if your program is correct,

and if not, give you some hints to fix it up.

5.Move forward:

let`s make arrow to move!

*from turtle imort **

forward(100)

when you run this code ,it makes the arrow to move forward! the

number is the how many step arrow want to move forward.

A bigger number will move the arrow further.

6.Task:

Make a move!:

Now it`s your turn to write your own turtle program!

write a program to make the arrow to move backward 100 steps.

it should look like it`s when you run it:

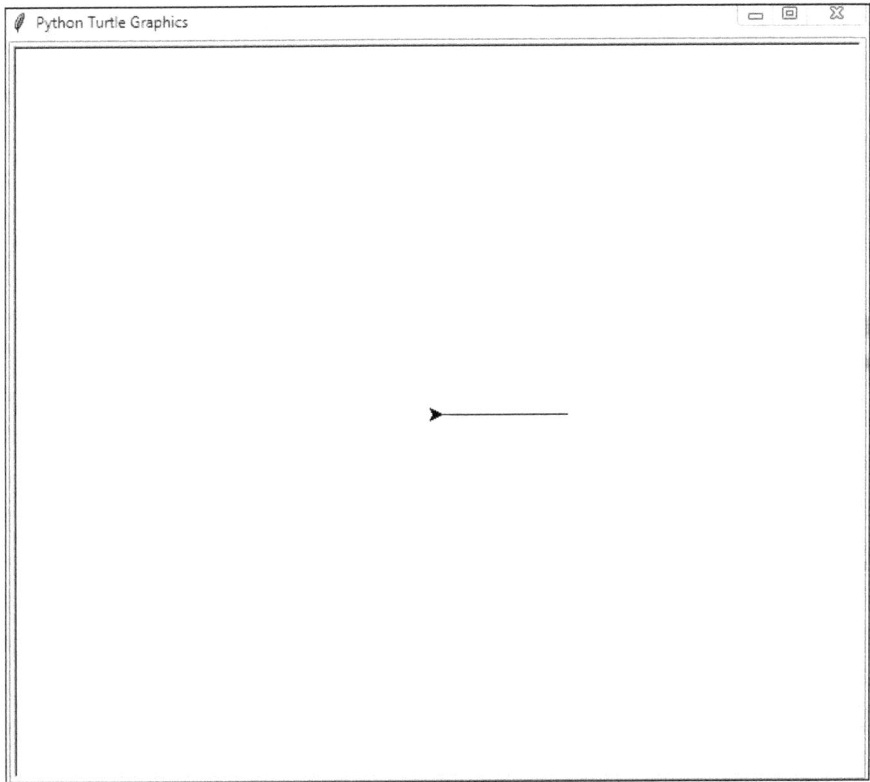

If you get confuse how to write this program go back few page and

read the basic turtle command

7.Angles with turtle:

What do these ° signs mean?

You can think of an angle as a change of direcon.

The angle between two lines is the turn you'd make to go from

one line to the other. Here, the lines are the turtle's old and new

directions.

Angles can be measured in degrees (wrien as °).

A 360° turn is a complete circle (a revolution).

Other turns are fracons of 360°.

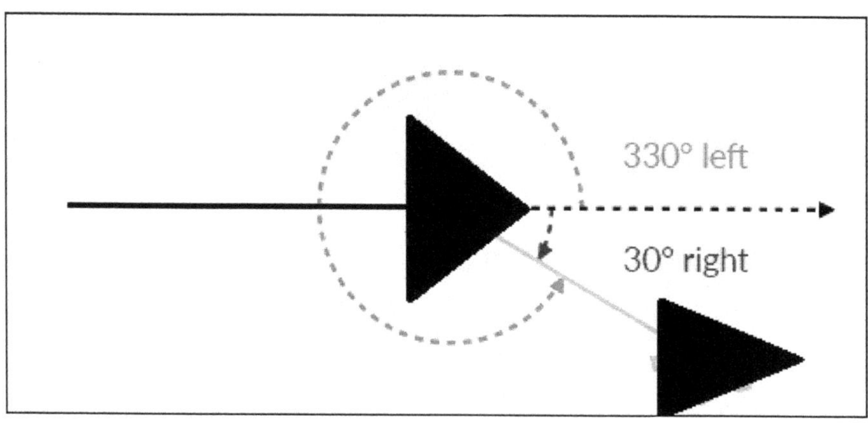

ANGLES

Turning a quarter of a circle (to face sideways) is 360° ÷ 4 = 90°.

This is called a right angle (don't confuse it with turning right!)

Turning half a circle (to face backwards) is 360° ÷ 2 = 180°.

This is called a straight angle (it looks like a straight line).

8.Turning corners:

The turtle always starts off facing to the right.

If you want to change which way the turtle is facing, you can turn

left or turn right.

These funtcion need the angle to turn in degrees.

Here we're turning left 90° (a right angle)

*from turtle import**

left(90)

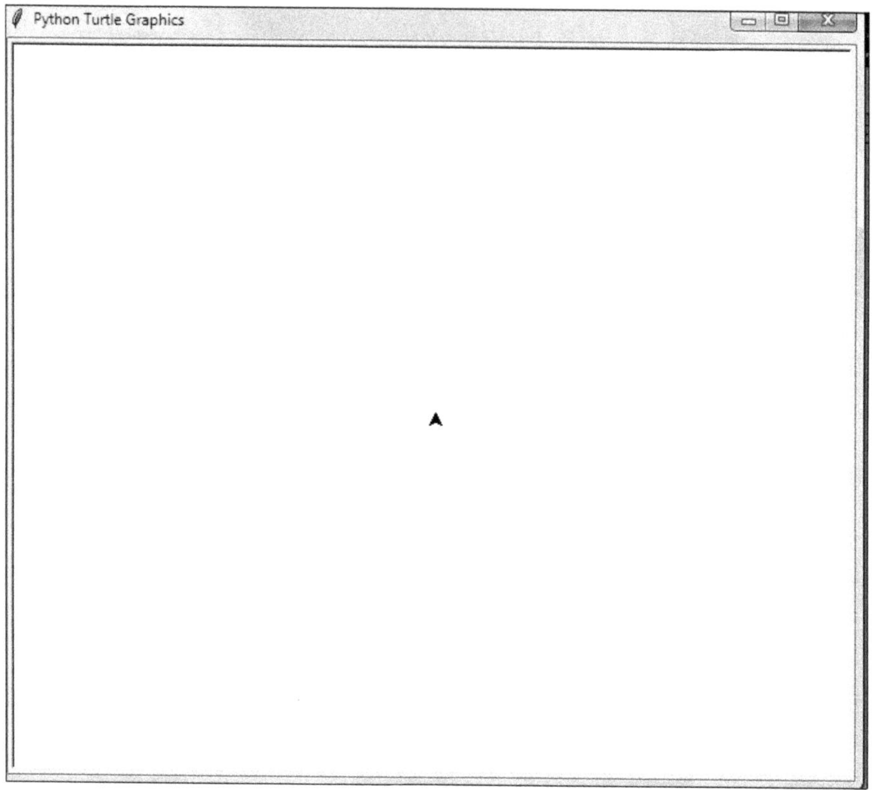

now the arrow is facing a top of the screen.

If you turn a total of 360° then the turtle will end up facing the same way as how it started, because 360° is a full circle.

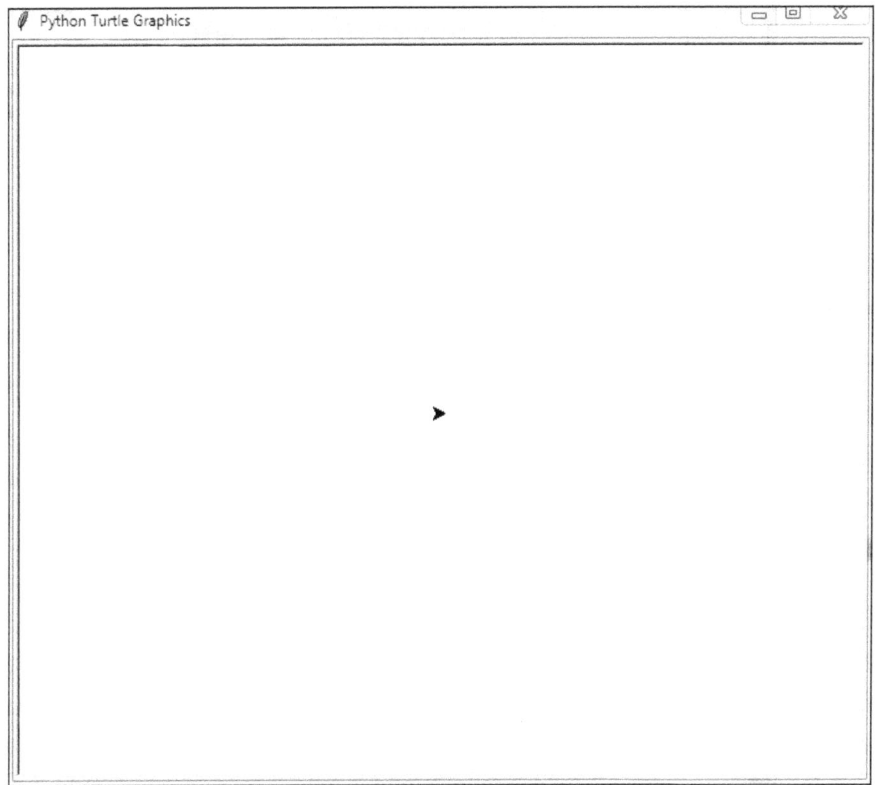

9.Drawing a shape:

The turtle follows instructions from its point of view.

If the turtle is facing right, calling forward will make the turtle move forward for it (but towards the right of the screen for you).

You can combine turtle instructions to draw shapes

*from turtle import**

forward(100)

right(120)

forward(100)

right(120)

forward(100)

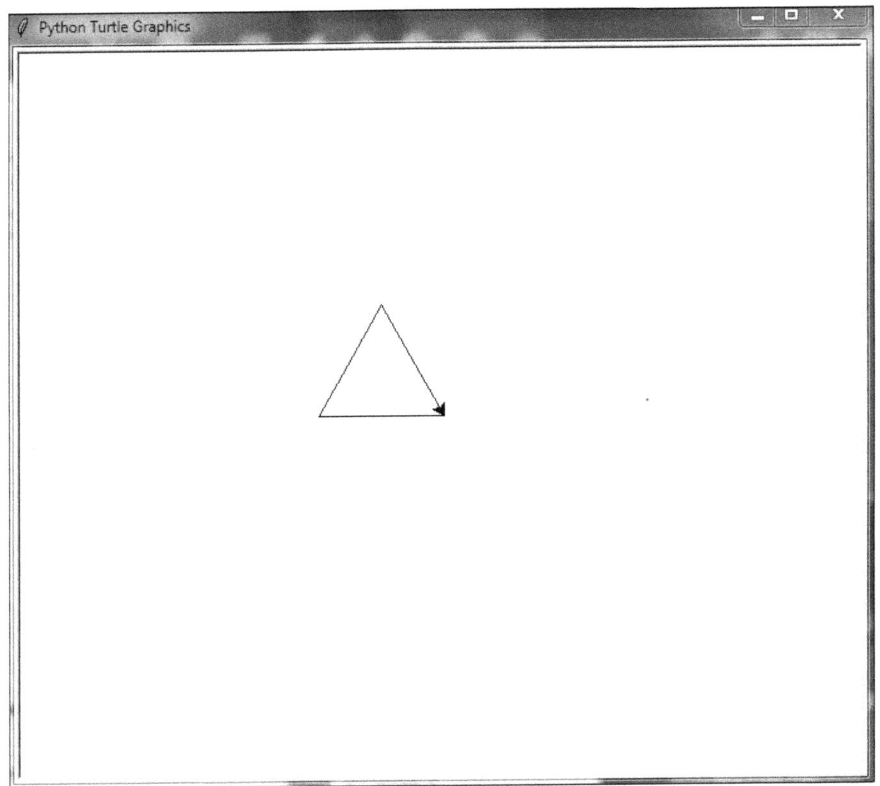

Here we've drawn a triangle with 60° angles, and 100 turtle steps

on each side.

Since the sides are equal length, we've drawn an equilateral

triangle.

10.task:

I`have given a part of program whuch tells the arrow to to draw a

square,your task is to finish it! when it`s finished, the arrow

should draw a square like this.

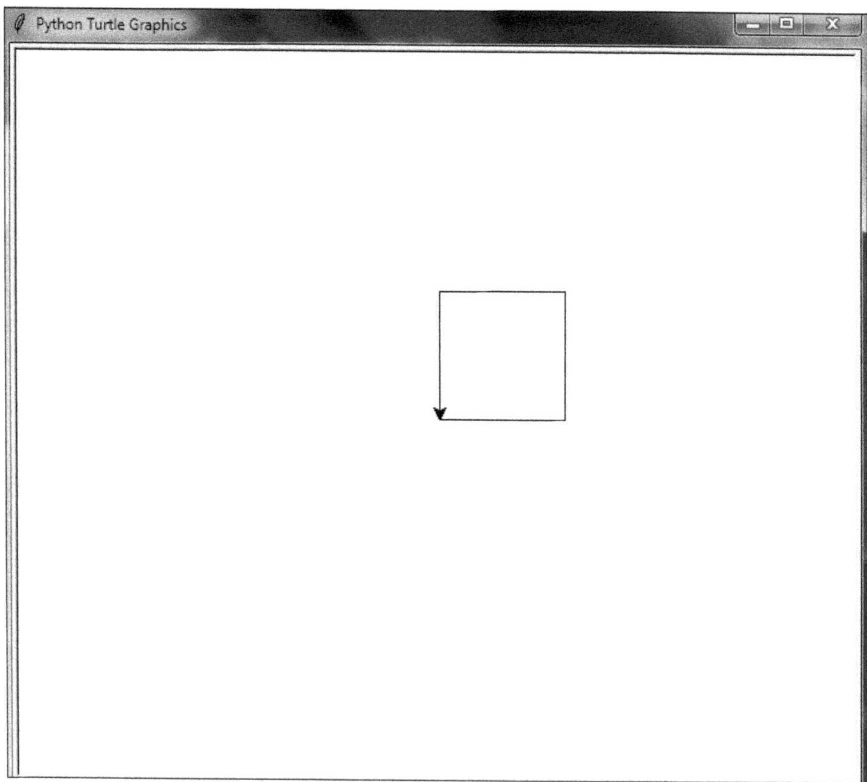

All sides of square should be 100 steps long.

11.Angles with the turtle:

Remember that you can think of an angles as achange of direction.

the angle between two lines inthe turn you`d make to go from one

line to other. Here,the lines of the turtle`s old and new direction.

We`ve add the green internal angles between the two lines in our

diagram. You can see the 180 degree - 150 - 30 turn you need.

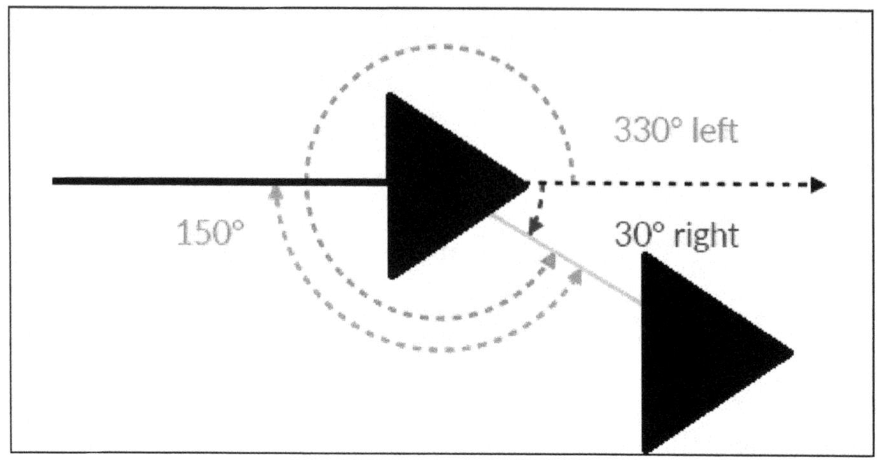

If you get confuse about the angle calculation, use the diagram

*from turtle import**

right(30)

forward(100)

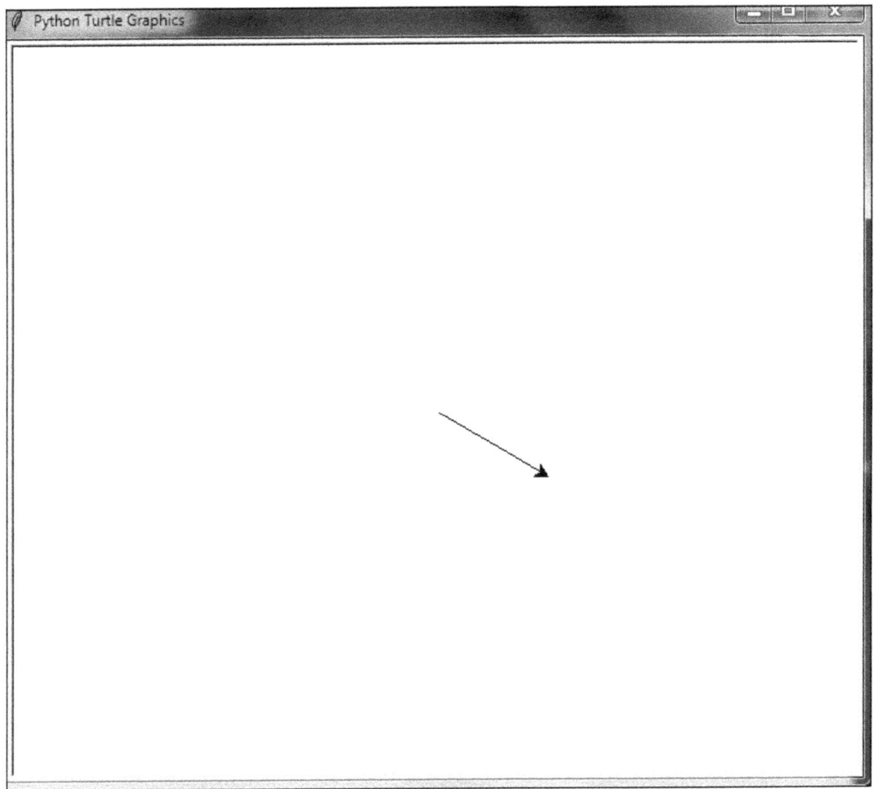

12.Looping with the turtle:

make shapes with using loop:

You have probably noticed that you repeat yourself a lot in the

turtle programs.

Using loops makes turtle much less respective!

drwaing a triangle in longway:

from turtle import *

forward(100)

right(120)

forward(100)

right(120)

forward(100)

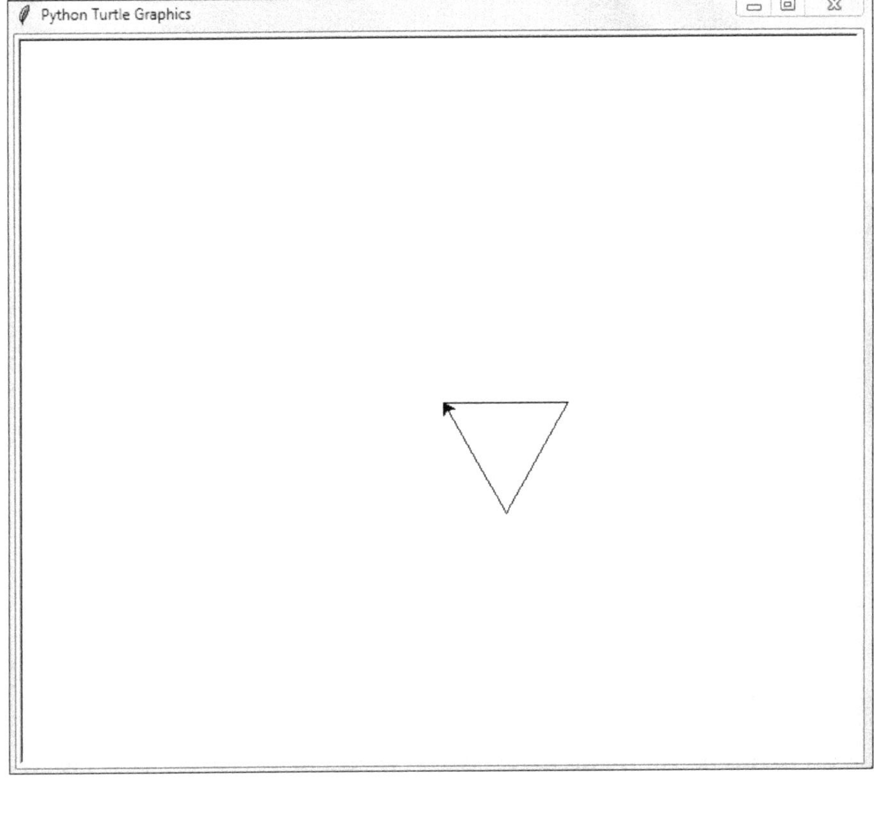

by using loop we don`t have to repeat the same two instruction

over and over again Here`s a shorter way of drawing a

triangle,using loops

*from turtle import**

for count in range(4):

forward(100)

right(120)

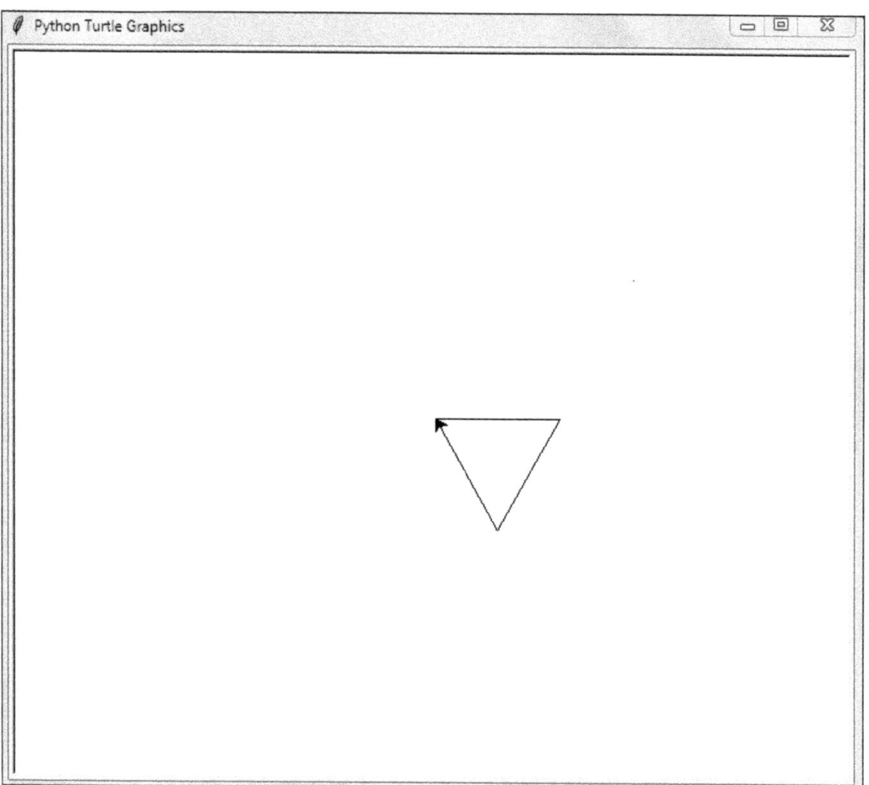

13.A closer look at loops:

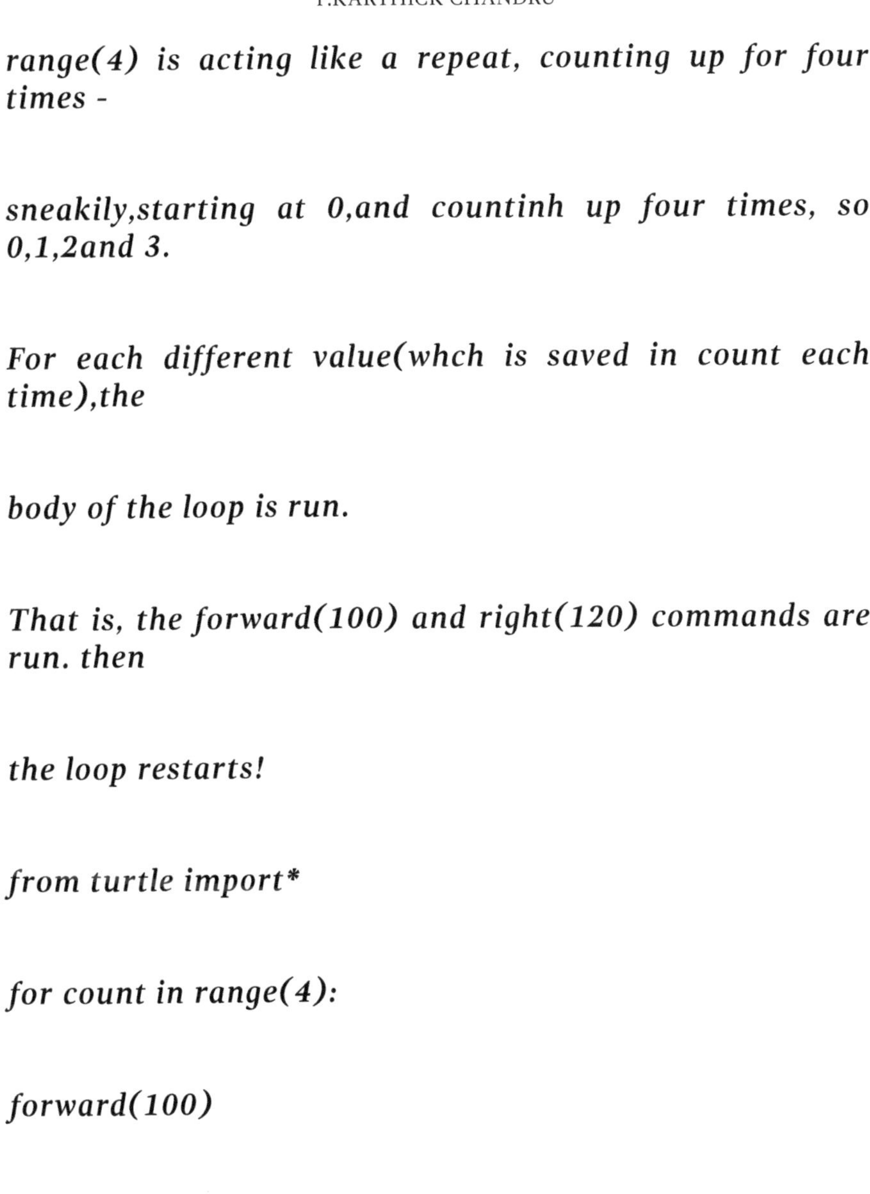

range(4) is acting like a repeat, counting up for four times -

sneakily,starting at 0,and countinh up four times, so 0,1,2and 3.

For each different value(whch is saved in count each time),the

body of the loop is run.

That is, the forward(100) and right(120) commands are run. then

the loop restarts!

```
from turtle import*

for count in range(4):

forward(100)

right(120)
```

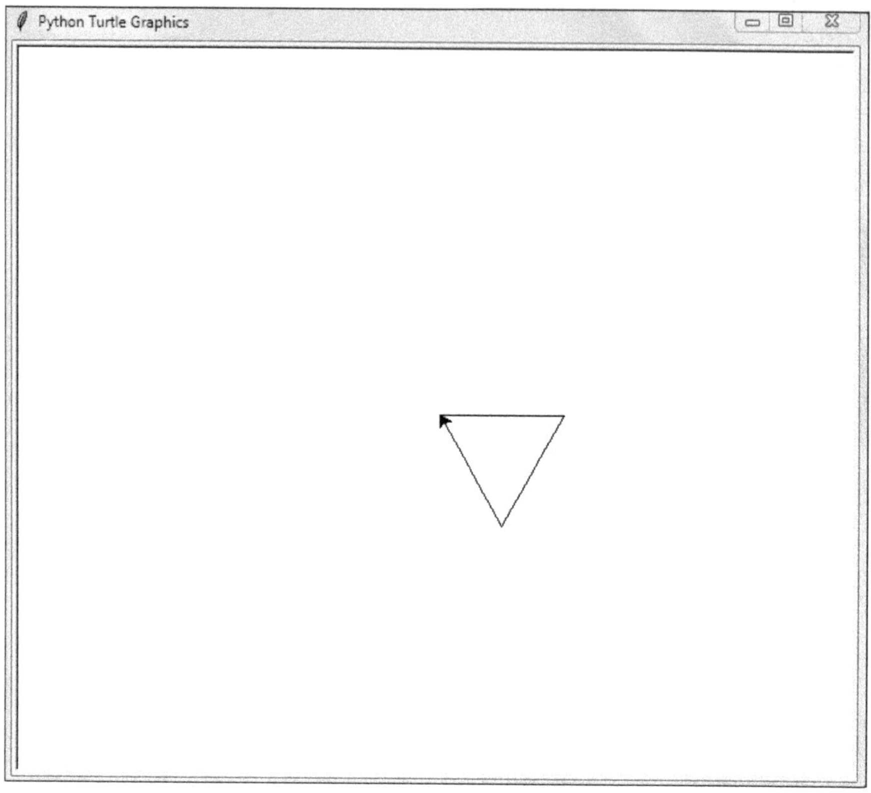

The body of the loop is all line that are intdented,- that is,that

start with two spaces in theexample above Make sure all the

instruction in your body are intdented to same amount! I

recommend to try two spaces.

14.Looping with numbers:

Just to see what`s happening,We can print out some informaion to

the screen.

this program will print out i love python to the screen four times.

for count in range(4):

print('i love python')

i love python

i love python

i love python

i love python

And this loop will print out the value that we`re saying in

count.

See how it gets set to a different number each time, first 0

then1,2and3.

```
>>> for count in range(6):
        print(count)


0
1
2
3
4
5
>>>
```

You don`t want to call it count,either! you can call it anything you

like.

for python in number(4):

print(python)

0

1

2

3

15.Looping and drawing:

let`s see how this work with the turtle!

```
>>> for side in range(4):
        print('now drawing side number')
        print(side)
        forward(50)
        right(90)


now drawing side number
0
now drawing side number
1
now drawing side number
2
now drawing side number
3
```

16.Looping lookouts!:

There are few gotchas with loops to look oaut for!

Dno`t forgot to type colon at the end of the for line it must end

with : orelse loop won`t work!

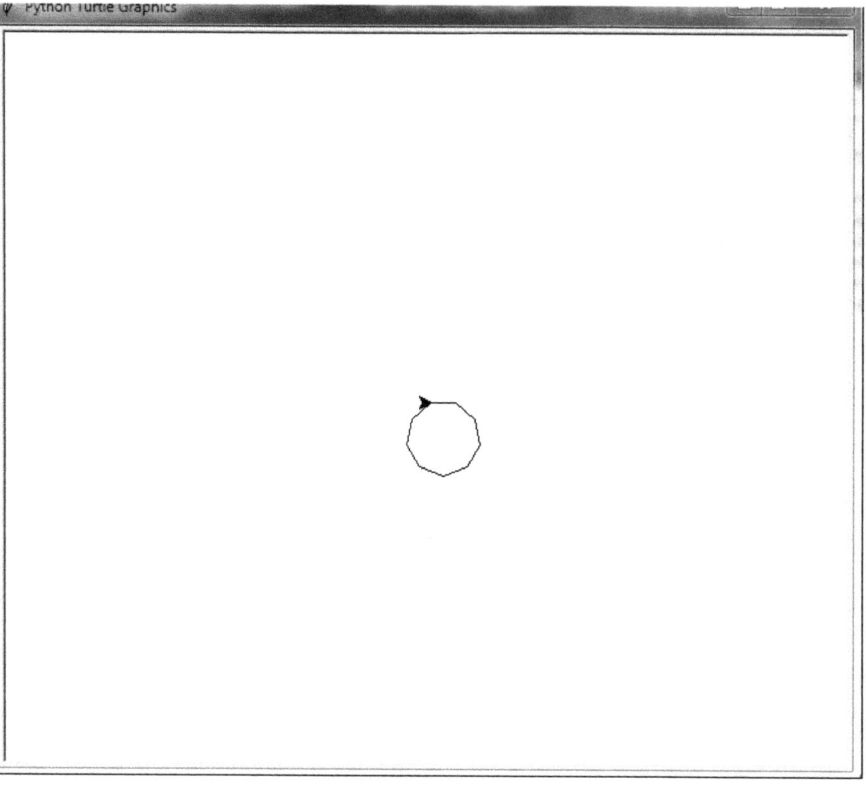

17.Loops and movement:

**** Repeat block:***

we can use for loop to create some fantastics pattens

```
from turtle import*

for count in range(7)

forward(50)

left(120)

forward(50)

left(120)

forward(50)

left(120)

left(60)
```

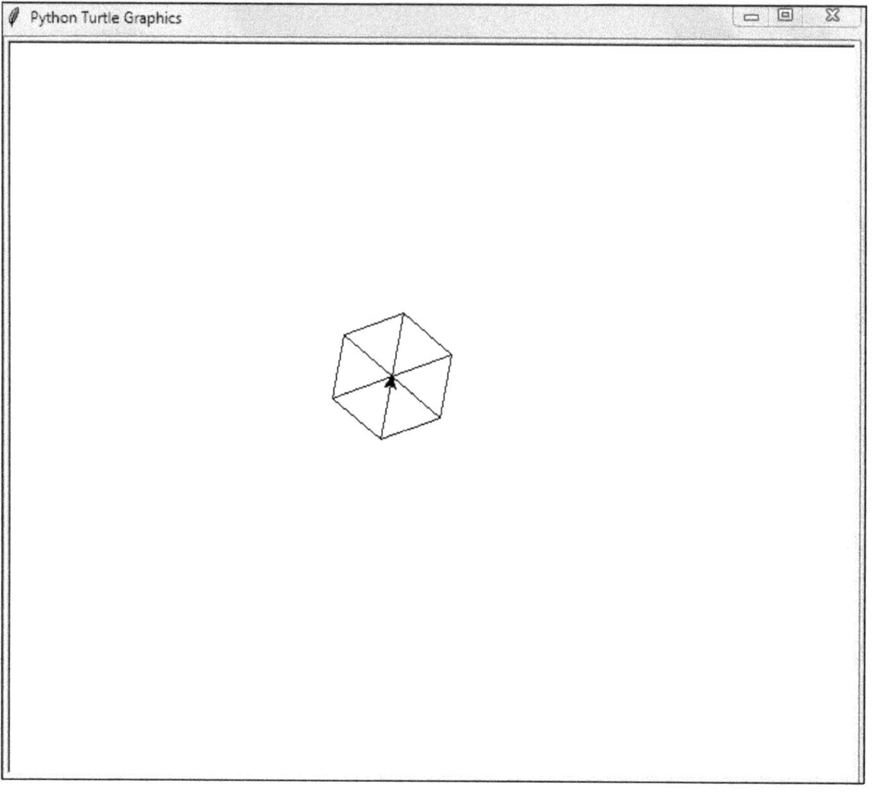

18.Squares on Squares on Squares:

When we use a for loop , it repeats everything indented inside of

it ,the so called body of the loop.

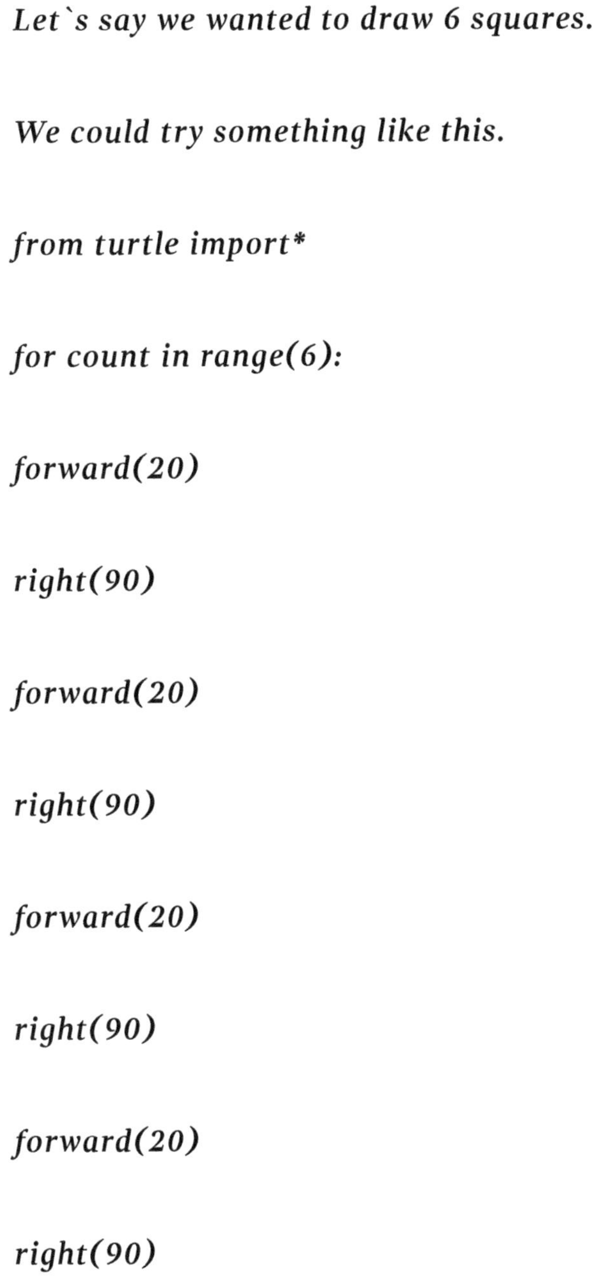

Let`s say we wanted to draw 6 squares.

We could try something like this.

```
from turtle import*

for count in range(6):

forward(20)

right(90)

forward(20)

right(90)

forward(20)

right(90)

forward(20)

right(90)
```

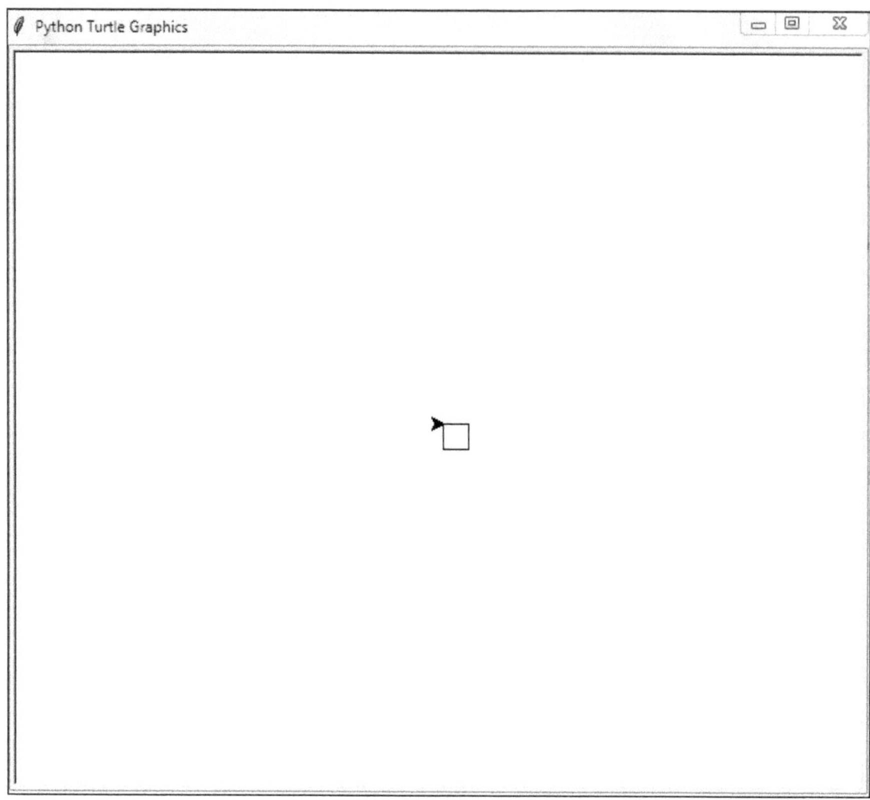

Six Squares are drawn,but top of each other!to draw more squares

side by side, we`ll need to add in an extra step to move forward

between each square.

19.Moving with loops:

Here we`ve added a left(90) at the beginning,and a forward(20)

at the end of the instructions within the for loop ,so that eah time

the square is drawn in a new position,pointing the right way.

left(90)

for count in range(6):

forward(20)

right(90)

forward(20)

right(90)

forward(20)

right(90)

forward(20)

right(90)

forward(20)

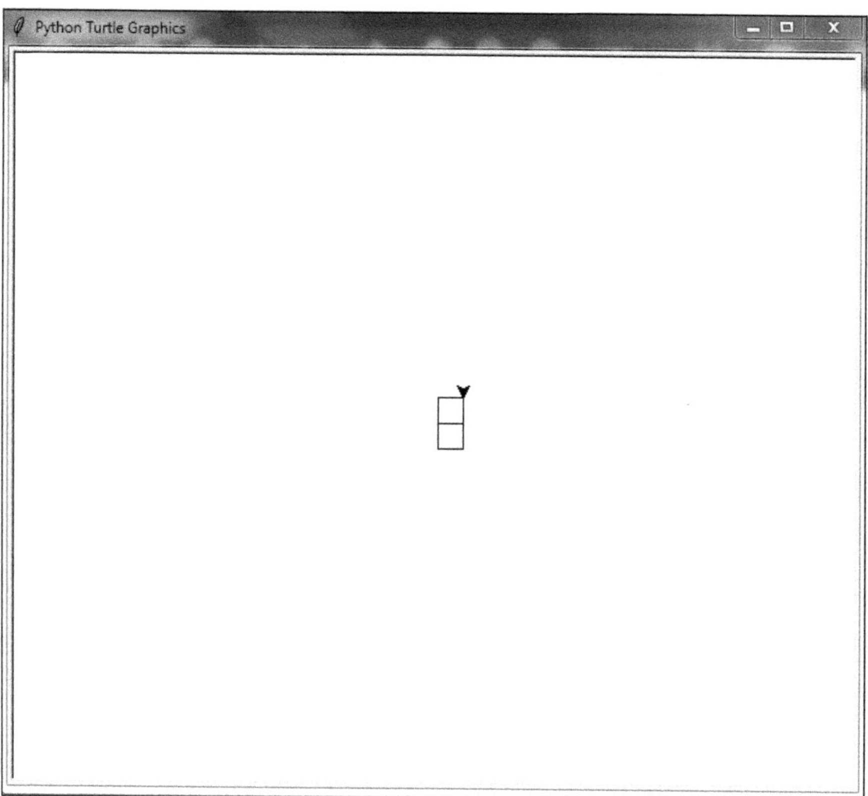

20.Let`s add a dash of colour:

*** Now with colour!**

Let`s add colour to the shapes!We can set the colour that we`re

drawing with using pencolor.

```
from turtle import*

pencolor('green')

forward(60)

left(120)

pencolor('yellowgreen')

forward(60)

left(120)

pencolor('violetred')

forward(60)
```

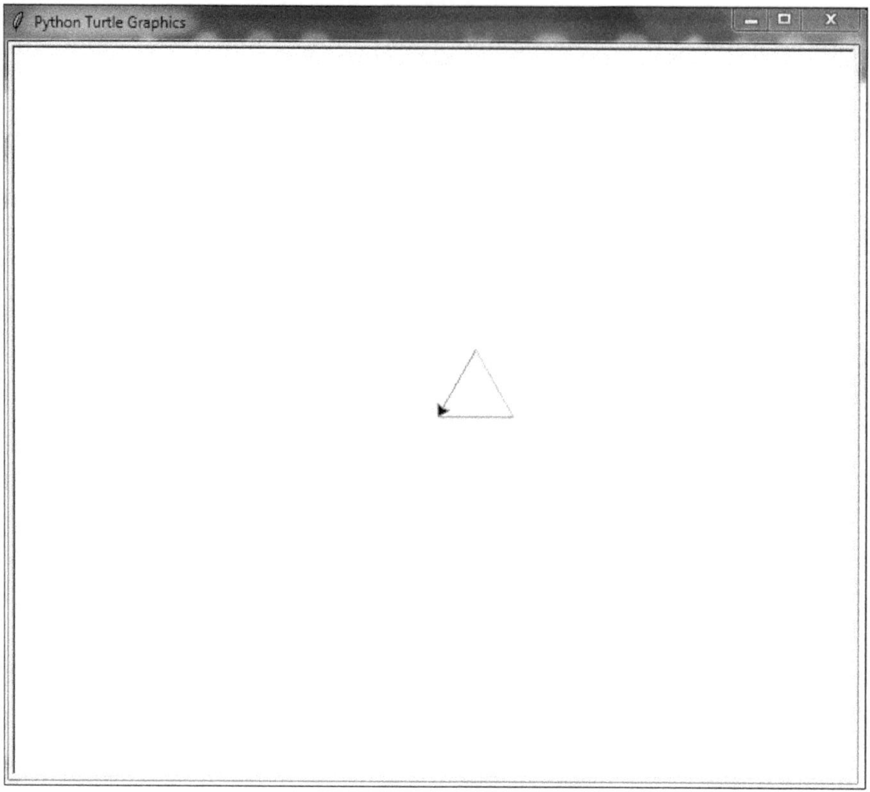

** most code uses color(American spelling)!*

Most program and modules(like turtle)will spell color with the

american spelling (c-o-l-o-r,no u) so watch out!

21.All the color of the rainbow:

Try some color names!But be carefull,you have use a color that

the turtle knows about, and you must spell it correctly.

azure	CornflowerBlue	DarkSlateGray4	honeydew2	LightGoldenrod3
azure1	cornsilk	DarkSlateGrey	honeydew3	LightGoldenrod4
azure2	cornsilk1	DarkTurquoise	honeydew4	LightGreen
azure3	cornsilk2	DarkViolet	HotPink	LightGrey
azure4	cornsilk3	DeepPink	HotPink1	LightPink
beige	cornsilk4	DeepPink1	HotPink2	LightPink1
bisque	cyan	DeepPink2	HotPink3	LightPink2
bisque1	cyan1	DeepPink3	HotPink4	LightPink3
bisque2	cyan2	DeepPink4	IndianRed	LightPink4
bisque3	cyan3	DeepSkyBlue	IndianRed1	LightSalmon
bisque4	cyan4	DeepSkyBlue1	IndianRed2	LightSalmon1
black	DarkBlue	DeepSkyBlue2	IndianRed3	LightSalmon2
blanchedalmond	DarkCyan	DeepSkyBlue3	IndianRed4	LightSalmon3
BlanchedAlmond	DarkGoldenrod	DeepSkyBlue4	ivory	LightSalmon4
blue	DarkGoldenrod1	DimGray	ivory1	LightSeaGreen
blue1	DarkGoldenrod2	DimGrey	ivory2	LightSkyBlue
blue2	DarkGoldenrod3	DodgerBlue	ivory3	LightSkyBlue1
blue3	DarkGoldenrod4	DodgerBlue1	ivory4	LightSkyBlue2
blue4	DarkGray	DodgerBlue2	khaki	LightSkyBlue3
BlueViolet	DarkGreen	DodgerBlue3	khaki1	LightSkyBlue4
brown	DarkGrey	DodgerBlue4	khaki2	LightSlateBlue

22.Turtle lines:

**** drawing thicker lines:***

Those lines are looking nice and colourful, but they're a bit thin!

We can change how thick the pen is using pensize.

The default pen width we have used so far is 1.

*from turtle import **

pensize(5)

forward(100)

left(90)

pensize(10)

forward(100)

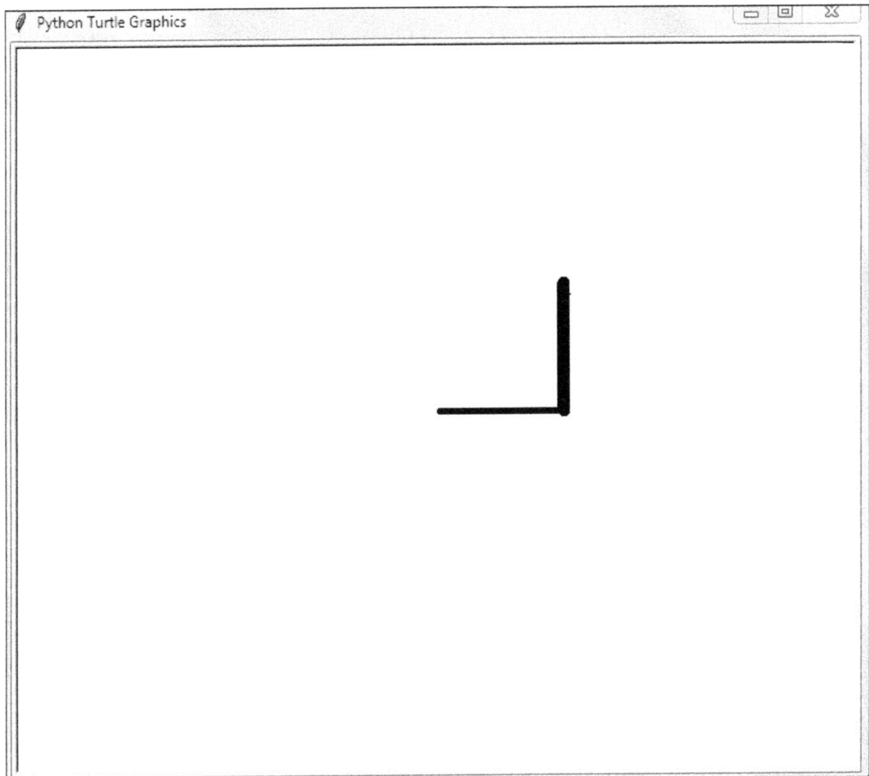

Try it out with different sizes!

23.Filled shapes with the color:

* *Filling with color:*

As well as changing the colour of lines, we can also fill shapes

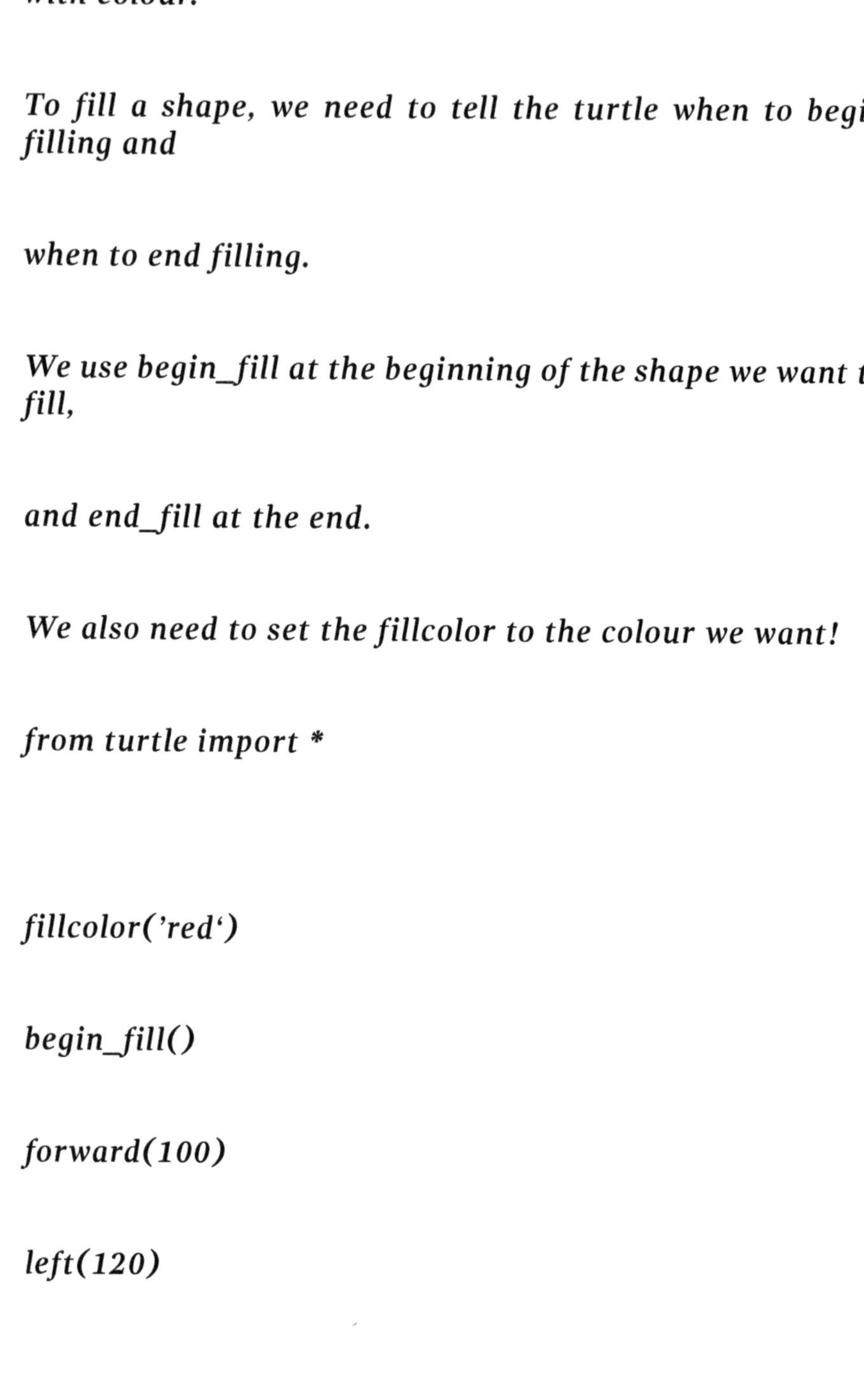

with colour.

To fill a shape, we need to tell the turtle when to begin filling and

when to end filling.

We use begin_fill at the beginning of the shape we want to fill,

and end_fill at the end.

We also need to set the fillcolor to the colour we want!

```
from turtle import *



fillcolor('red')

begin_fill()

forward(100)

left(120)
```

forward(100)

left(120)

forward(100)

left(120)

end_fill()

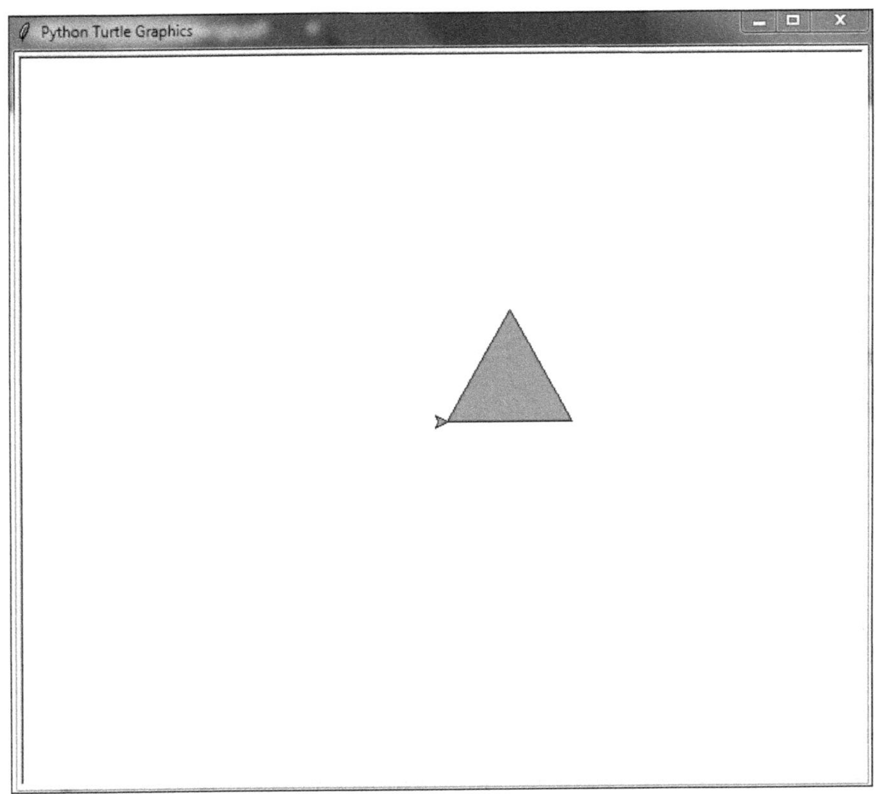

Try to gusses what is the output of this program before seeing the

example! and try to change the fill color.

24.loops and fills:

We`ve already seen how to draw shapes with loops,let`s draw

some shapes with both loops and fills.

```
from turtle import *

fillcolor('cornflowerblue‘)

begin_fill()

for count in range(4):

forward(100)

left(90)
```

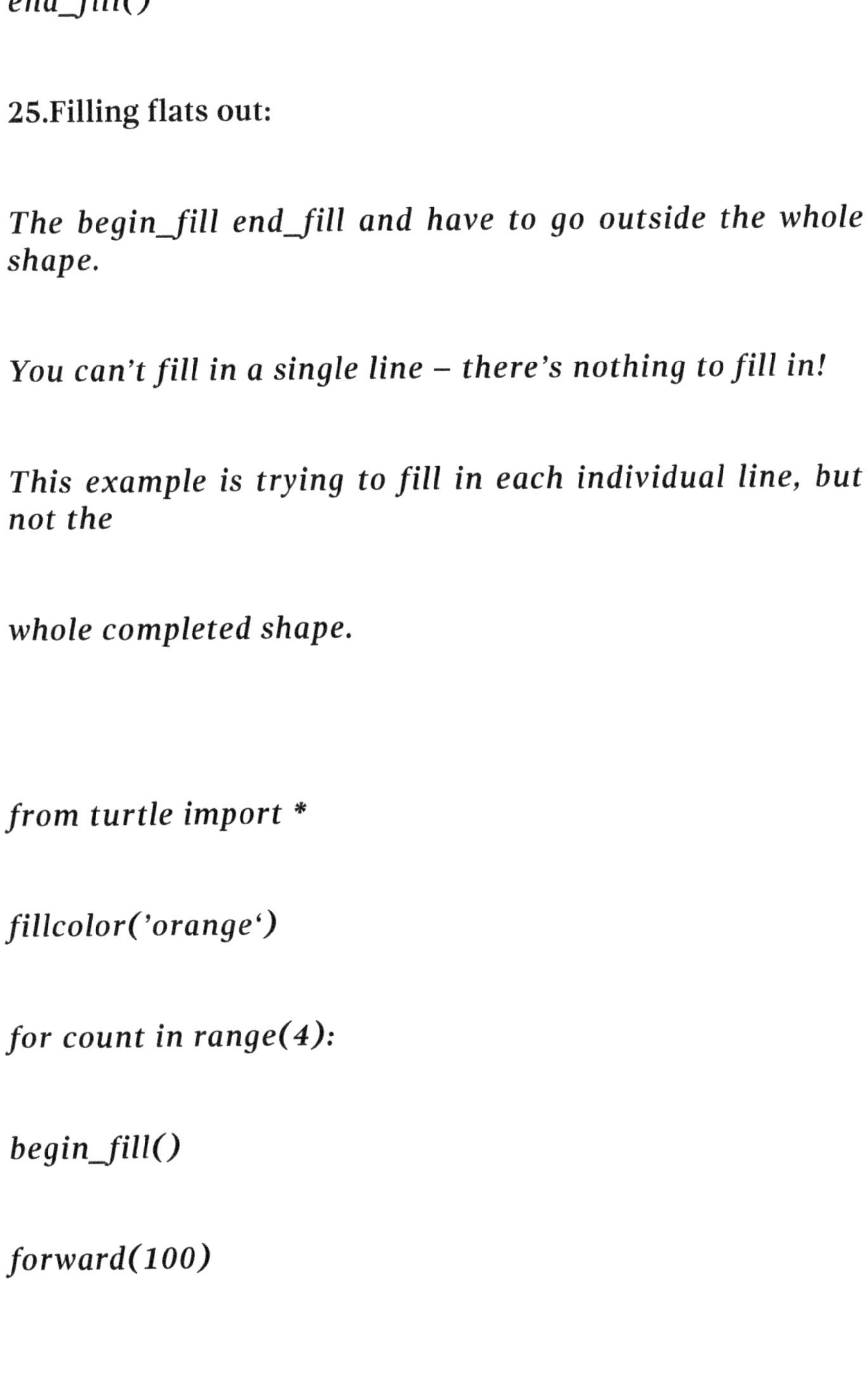

```
end_fill()
```

25.Filling flats out:

The begin_fill end_fill and have to go outside the whole shape.

You can’t fill in a single line – there’s nothing to fill in!

This example is trying to fill in each individual line, but not the

whole completed shape.

```
from turtle import *

fillcolor(’orange‘)

for count in range(4):

begin_fill()

forward(100)
```

left(90)

end_fill()

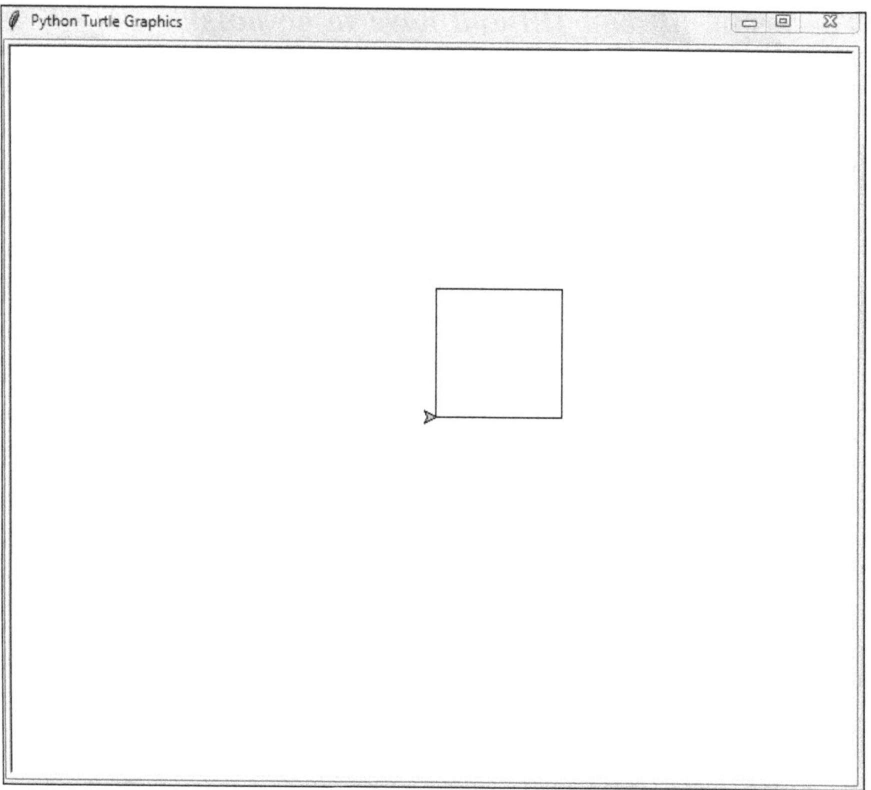

See how the shape isn't coloured in?

If we put the fill inside the loop, then the turtle tries to separately fill each side of the shape, which doesn't work!

26.Functional filling:

The begin_fill and end_fill and need to be wrapped around

the whole shape you want to fill in.

In this case, that means putting them outside the for loop.

```
from turtle import *

fillcolor('orange')

begin_fill()

for count in range(4):

forward(100)

left(90)

end_fill()
```

27.Advance turtle-fu!:

** background color:*

it`s any boring to always have a plain white background this code

for you.

that`s why we`ve way to set color bgcolor it is short form

of background color.

*from turtle import **

bgcolor('red')

28.variables and imput:

** python the calculator:*

Computer can do billions of calculation per seconds! the computers are really good at, working with numbers.

python have variables like calculator so, python is better than

calculator.

We can use variables to store numbers for later, and we can do

calculations on them, too! Python can do all the operaons you

expect from a calculator...

name calculator python

Addition +

Subtract - -

*Multiply × **

divison ÷ /

29.recalling once again:

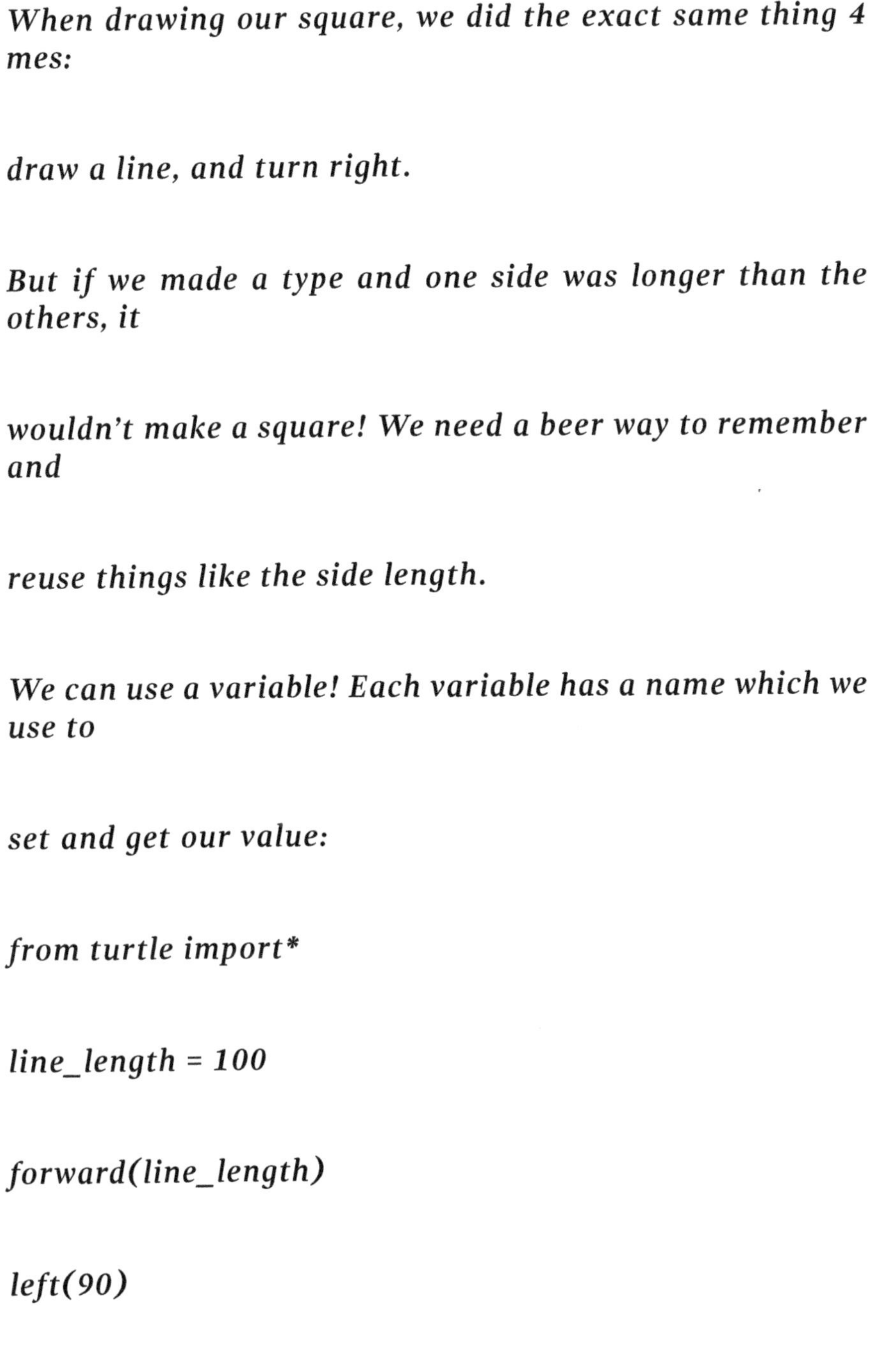

When drawing our square, we did the exact same thing 4 mes:

draw a line, and turn right.

But if we made a type and one side was longer than the others, it

wouldn't make a square! We need a beer way to remember and

reuse things like the side length.

We can use a variable! Each variable has a name which we use to

set and get our value:

```
from turtle import*

line_length = 100

forward(line_length)

left(90)
```

forward(line_length)

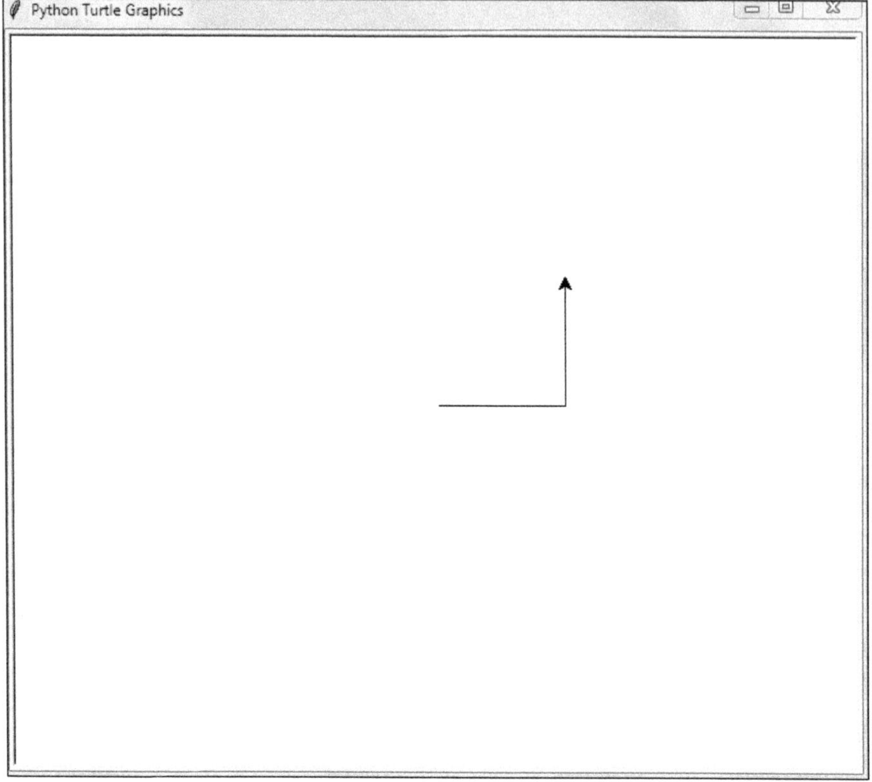

line_length = 100 creates a new variable called line_length. It

holds the value100.

We can then use the line_length variable to use that number as

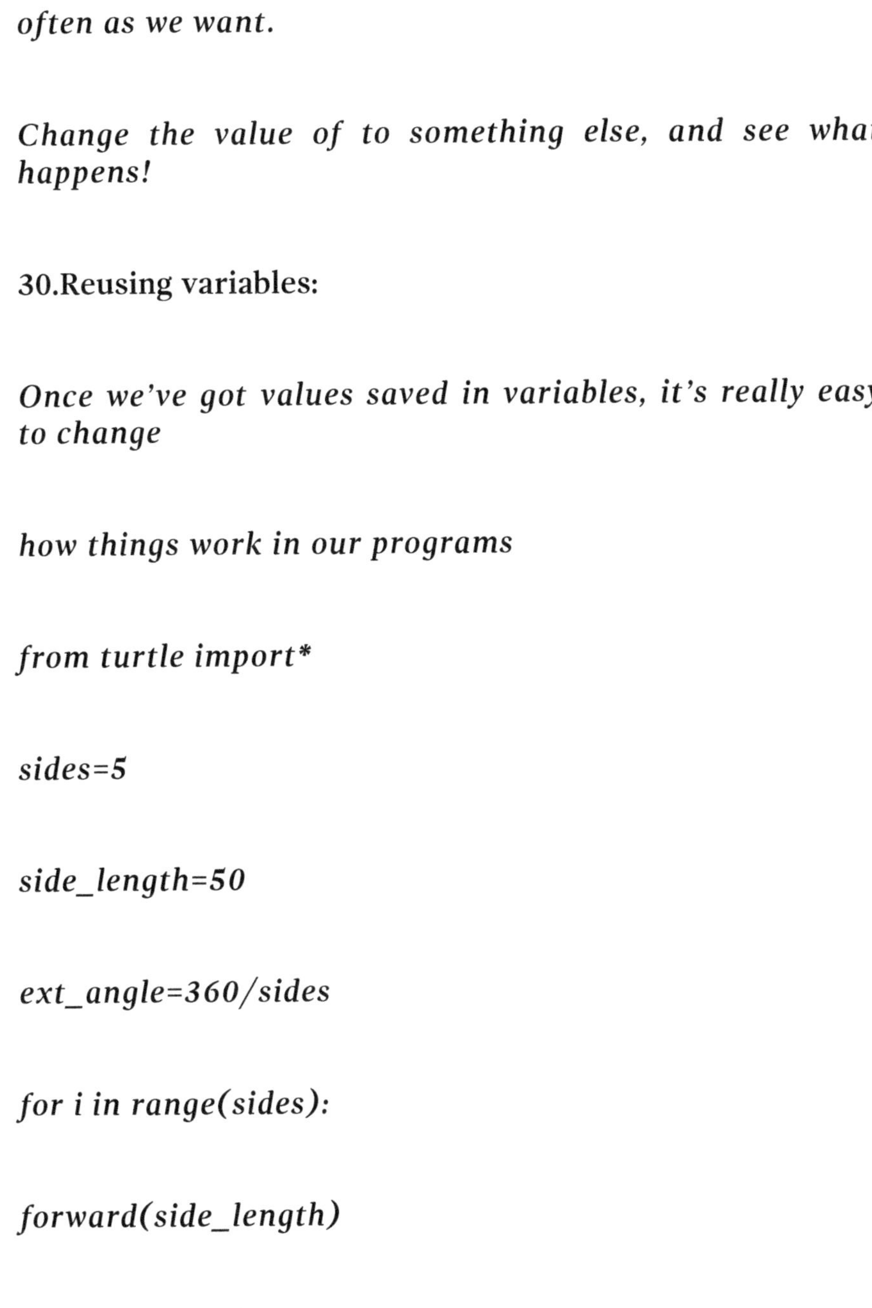

often as we want.

Change the value of to something else, and see what happens!

30.Reusing variables:

Once we've got values saved in variables, it's really easy to change

how things work in our programs

```
from turtle import*

sides=5

side_length=50

ext_angle=360/sides

for i in range(sides):

forward(side_length)

left(ext_angle)
```

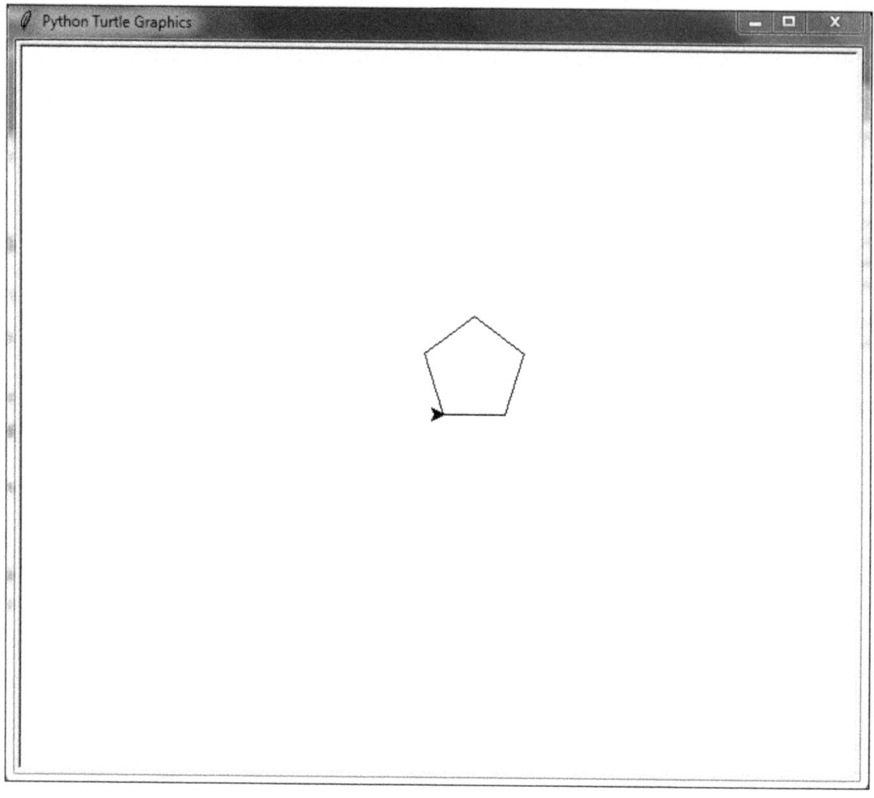

31.Asking question:

We can use input to get the computer to ask a question.

We might want to know what the user's favourite colour is. We

could ask like this fave_colour = input("What is your favourite colour? ") print("You answered: " + fave_colour)

try running this few times and saying different colors.

32. numbers and strings are different things:

Computers understand informaon in a different way to how

people understand informaon.

Humans can easily understanding that the spoken word "dog", a

picture of a dog, or the leters d, o and g all represent the same

thing.

Computers don't see these similaries - they only see differences.

This is especially important when dealing with numbers!

If we ask a question with the computer using input, the answer

always comes back as a word - what we call a string (short for

string of characters).

If we want to use the answer that the user tells us as a number, we

need to make sure Python understands it as a number.

We can do this using int

```
from turtle import *

side_length = input("How long should the square sides be? ")

side_length = int(side_length)

for i in range(4):

forward(side_length)
```

right(90)

33.Asking user for information:

The turtle functions, like forward, only work with numbers.

So if we ask the user for informaon using input, if it's a number,we

need to make sure we use int to save it as a number.

*from turtle import **

distance = input('How far? ')

forward(distance)

Because we're calling forward with 50 (a string), instead of 50 (an

integer), it complains with a TypeError:

```
How far? 50
Traceback (most recent call last):
  File "program.py", line 3, in <module>
    forward(distance)
  File "/tmp/tmpbgmiSJ/turtle.py", line 632, in forward
    raise TypeError('Expected integer or float argument')
TypeError: Expected integer or float argument
```

Wow, this looks scary, but it isn't! Look at the last line. It says the

TypeError occurred in our call to forward line 3 of program.py

(our code).

The forward function is defined in turtle.py (the turtle module

file).

Notice that where the error is detected isn't where the mistake

was made (the missing int). This is very common in

programming.

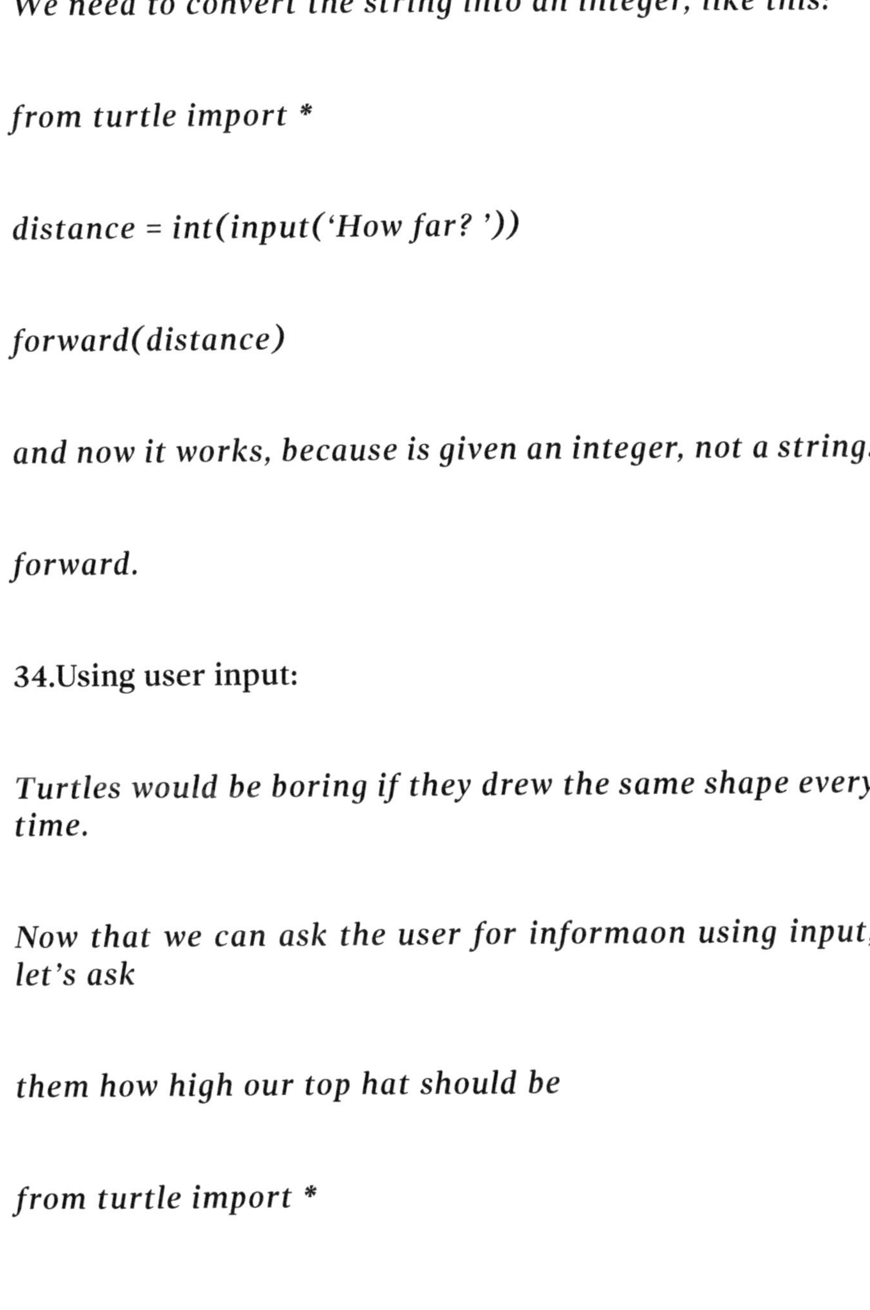

We need to convert the string into an integer, like this:

*from turtle import **

distance = int(input('How far? '))

forward(distance)

and now it works, because is given an integer, not a string.

forward.

34.Using user input:

Turtles would be boring if they drew the same shape every time.

Now that we can ask the user for informaon using input, let's ask

them how high our top hat should be

*from turtle import **

hat_height = int(input('What height should the hat be? '))

forward(30)

left(90)

forward(hat_height)

right(90)

forward(30)

right(90)

forward(hat_height)

left(90)

forward(30)

35.Making decision:

** why do we need decisions?*

So far our programs have been just a sequence of steps that run

from top to bottm.

Theprograms run the same way every me.

In the real world, we decide to take different steps based on our

situaon.

For example, if it`s raining , we do an extra step of wearing

a jerkin before leaving the office.

This flowchart discribe this process(or Algorithm):

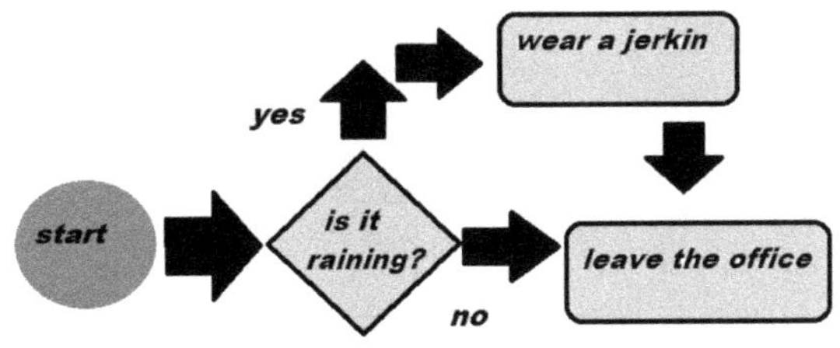

Flow chart

The dimonds needs a yes or no decision. if the answer is yes , we

do extra step of wearing a jerkin if the answer is no we can skip

it.

36. What if it is raining?

let`s write a python program with using the above flowchart:

raining = input('Is it raining (yes/no)? ')

if raining == 'yes':

print('wear a jerkin.')

print('Leave the office.')

Try it! What happens when you say yes, no, or any other answer?

Notice that the first print is indented (by two spaces).

The print instruction is used to display characters and text on the

screen.

If the value stored in raining is equal to 'yes' (because the user

entered yes), then the body is run.

Otherwise, it is skipped. The second print always runs, because it

is not indented, and isn't controlled by the if statement.

37.Decisions with turtle:

we can use if statement to make decisions with the turtle, too!

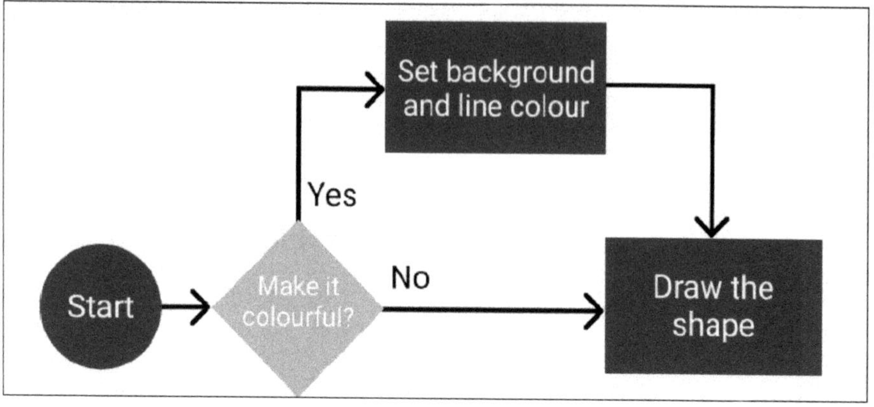

flowchart for making colourful image with the turtle

*from turtle import **

colourful = input('Make it colourful? ')

if colourful == 'yes':

bgcolor('yellow')

pencolor('darkgreen')

forward(50)

38. Controlling the block of code:

Now i going to ask one question the statement which control

more than one statement is called _________.

the answer is if statement.

These statements must have the same indentation like this:

*from turtle import **

colourful = input('Make it colourful? ')

if colourful == 'yes':

bgcolor('yellow')

pencolor('darkgreen')

pensize(5)

forward(50)

If the user types in "yes" then all the indented lines (the block)

will be executed first, then continue on with the rest of the

program.

If it's anything else, those lines will be skipped and the next not-

indented line (forward(50)) will be executed.

39.Assingment vs comparison:

You will notice in our examples that we are using two equals signs

to check whether the variable is equal to a particular value:

colourful = input("Draw a background? ")

if colourful == 'yes':

bgcolor('yellow')

this seems quite confusing for beginner.

a single = is used for assingment This is what we do to set

variables.

The first line of the program above is setting the variable

colourful to the value "yes" using a single equals

sign.

A double == is used for comparison.

This is what we do to check whether two things are equal. The

second line of the program above is checking whether the variable

is equal to "yes" using a double colourful equals sign. if you

accindentally mix these up , the python will help by giving you a SytaxError.

for example try this program:

colourful = input("Draw a background? ")

if colourful = "yes":

bgcolor("yellow")

the second line only has one equal sing where it should have two.

40.Decisions with two option:

if statements allow you to make yes or no decisions. In Python

these are called False and True Sometimes, we want an extra part

to the if statement which is only run when a condtion is False.

if the user says 'yes' if i have 10$, then the program should say to

buy pizza,but otherwise it should say to buy candy.

41. if there is no pizza:

In Python the else keyword specifies the steps to follow if

the condition is False.(in this case if there is no pizza)

if the user says yes if i have 10$ then the first block is

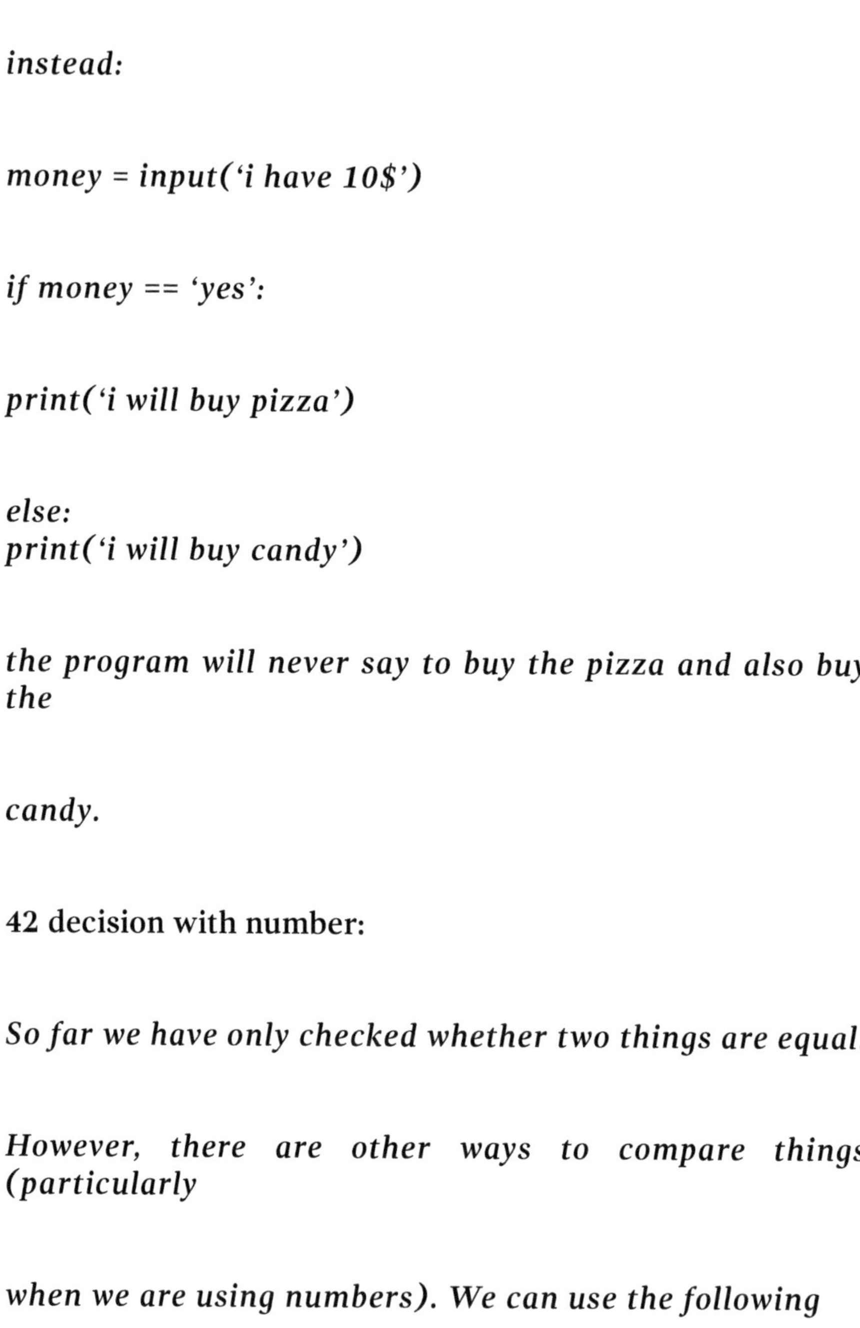

executed,otherwise, the second block is executed

instead:

money = input('i have 10$')

if money == 'yes':

print('i will buy pizza')

else:
print('i will buy candy')

the program will never say to buy the pizza and also buy the

candy.

42 decision with number:

So far we have only checked whether two things are equal.

However, there are other ways to compare things (particularly

when we are using numbers). We can use the following

comparison operators in ifstatements:

operation operator

equal to ==

not equal to !=

less than <

less than or equal to <=

greater than >

greater than or equal to >=

you can use a print statement to test these operators in conditional expressions.

a=3

print(a<9)

true

this print ture because 3 is less than 9

a=3

print(a>9)

false

this print false because 3 is greater than 9

43 expermenting with comparison:

type the first two line Let's try some more examples to

demonstrate how condtional operators work. Firstly, we have less

than or equal to (<=)

a = 5

print (a <= 5)

true

Any value of a up to and including 10 will result in True.Any

value of a greater than 10 will result in False.

The opposite is true for greater than or equal to (>=). Another

important operator is not equal to (!=)

a = 5

print (a ! = 10)

true

Notice this program prints true because 5 is not equal to 10. This

can be a bit confusing - see what happens if you change the value of a to 10.

44 creating decisions with numbers :

Now we can bring together everything we've learned in this

section, and write programs that make decisions based on

numerical input. The example below makes two decisions based

on the value in x.

a = 5

if a <= 5:

print('a is less than or equal to five')

else:

print('a is greater than or equal to five')

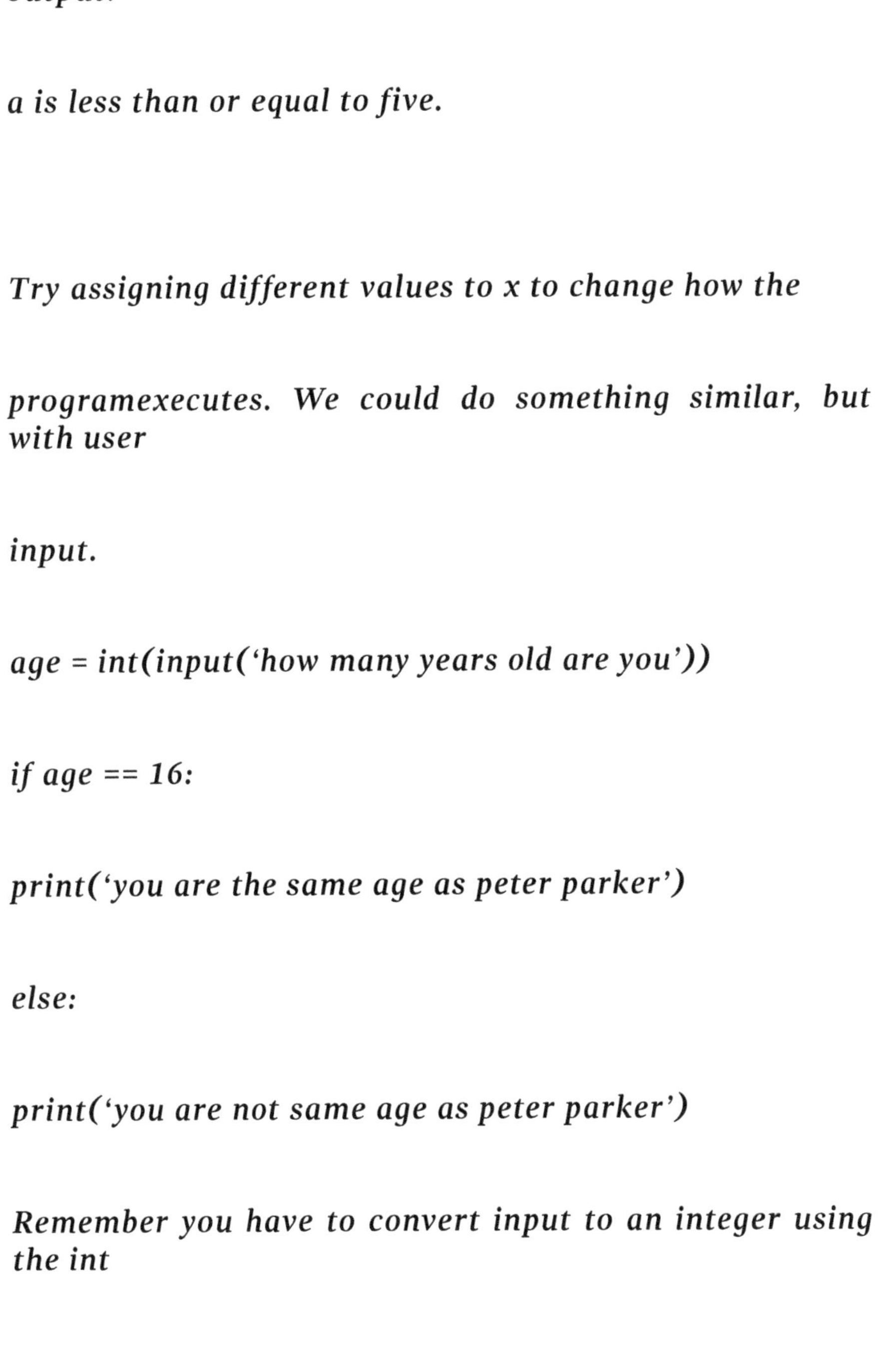

output:

a is less than or equal to five.

Try assigning different values to x to change how the

programexecutes. We could do something similar, but with user

input.

```
age = int(input('how many years old are you'))

if age == 16:

print('you are the same age as peter parker')

else:

print('you are not same age as peter parker')
```

Remember you have to convert input to an integer using the int function if you want to do numerical comparisons.

45 creating complex decision:

Sometimes, we want to make decisions with more than two

options. We can use elif short for else if to compare multiple

things in the same check.

mark = input('what is mark in maths')

if mark == '100':

print('you scored fabulous mark')

elif mark == '90':

print('you scored good mark')

elif mark == '40':

print ('you scored just pass')

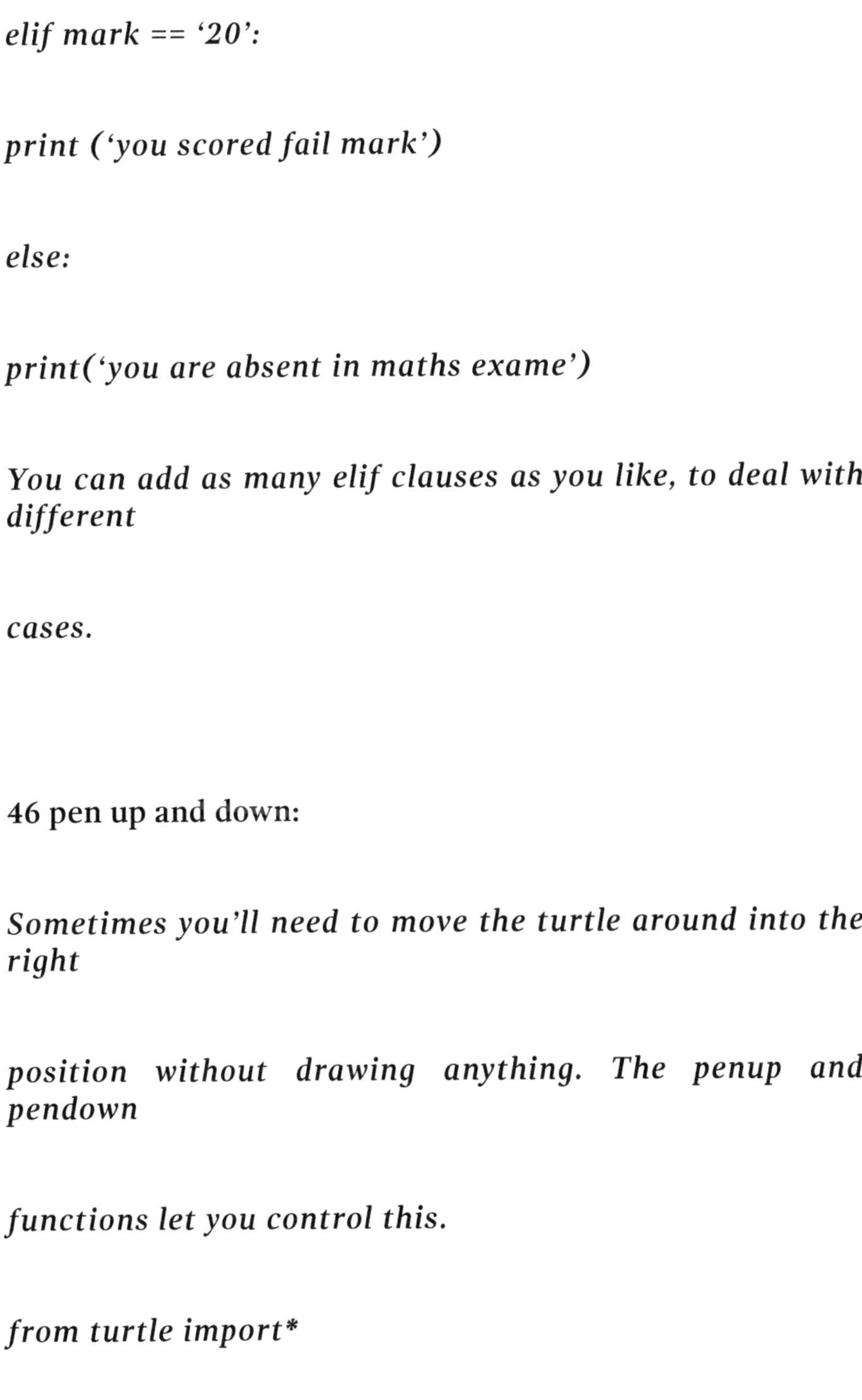

elif mark == ‘20’:

print (‘you scored fail mark’)

else:

print(‘you are absent in maths exame’)

You can add as many elif clauses as you like, to deal with different

cases.

46 pen up and down:

Sometimes you’ll need to move the turtle around into the right

position without drawing anything. The penup and pendown

functions let you control this.

*from turtle import**

forward (50)

penup

forward (50)

pendown

forward (50)

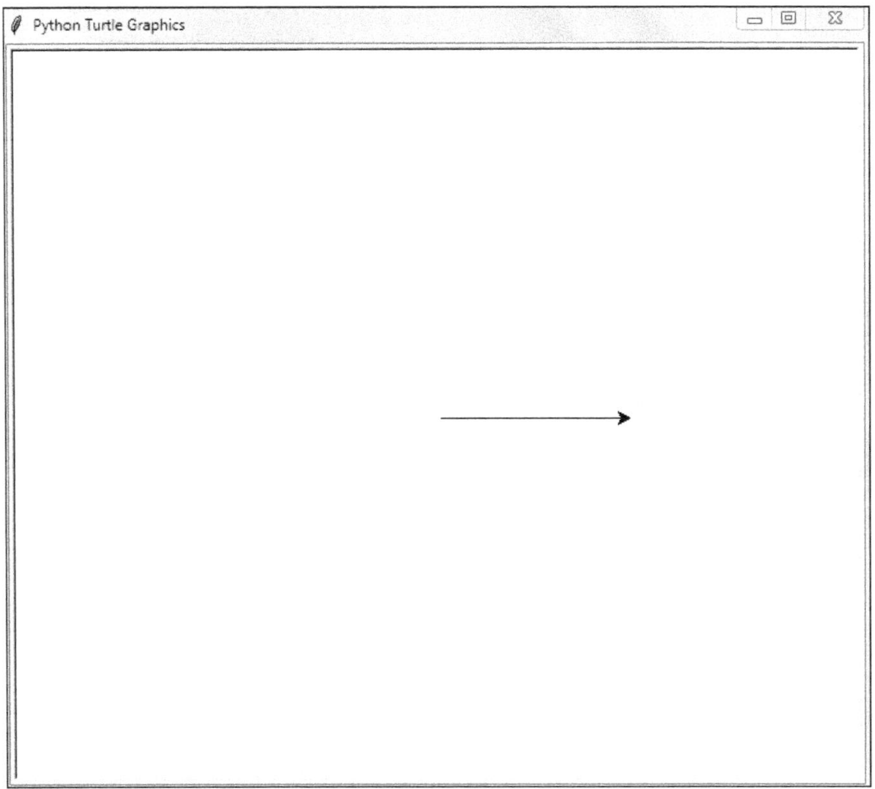

Imagine the turtle is holding a pen, after you've lifted up the pen

with penup the pen is off the paper and the turtle won't draw

anything as it moves around. After you've put the pen back down

with pendown, the turtle will draw as it moves again.

47 challenges:

starting from square one:

your task is draw a square when you finish this task the turtle

should draw like this.

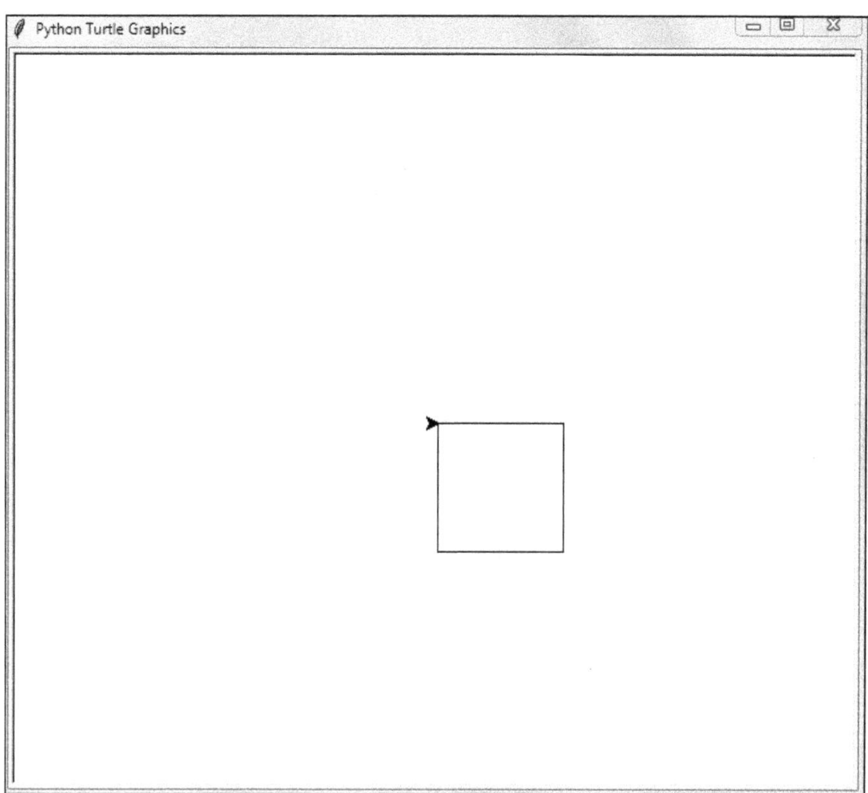

* get rect!:

write a turtle program to draw a rectangle, with a width (top and

bottom sides) of 120 turtle steps and height(the left and right

sides) of 50 turtle steps. the output of your program should like

this.

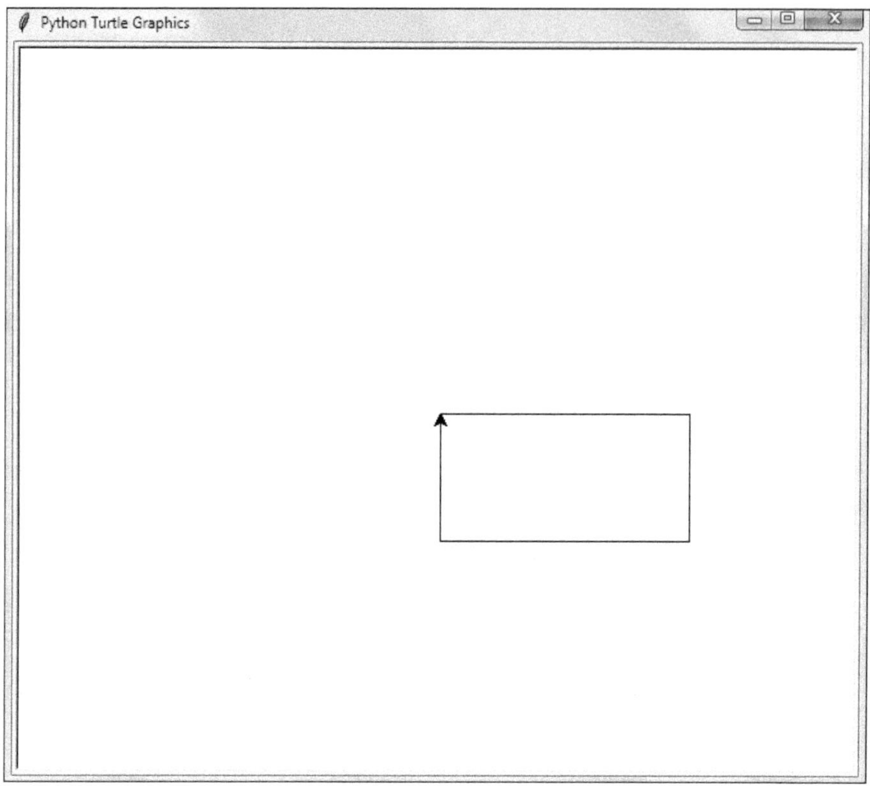

***draw domino:**

write a program to draw a domino made up of two square on top

of the other. each side of each square should be 50 turtle steps

long.

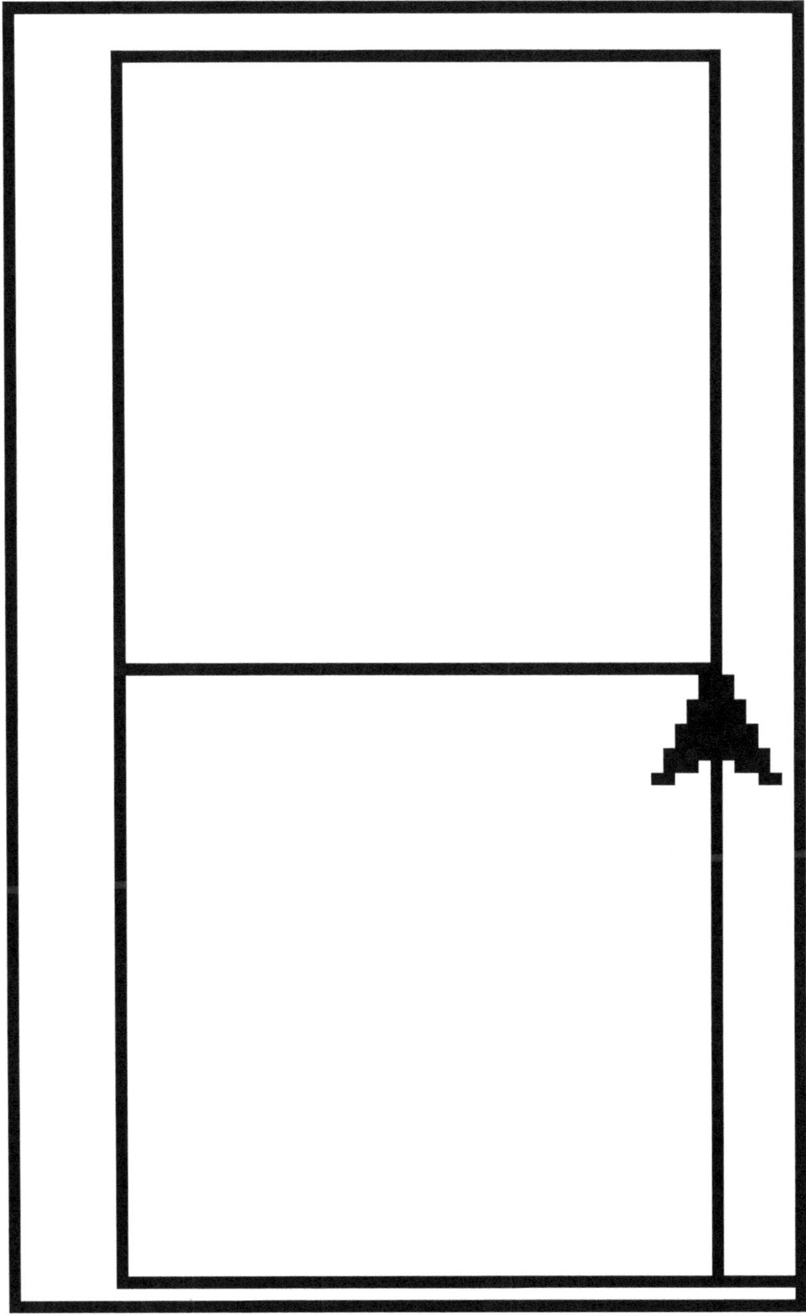

*** equilateral triangle:**

write a tirtle to draw a equilateral triangle with the sides being

100 turtle steps long all angle in equilateral triangle are 60 degree.

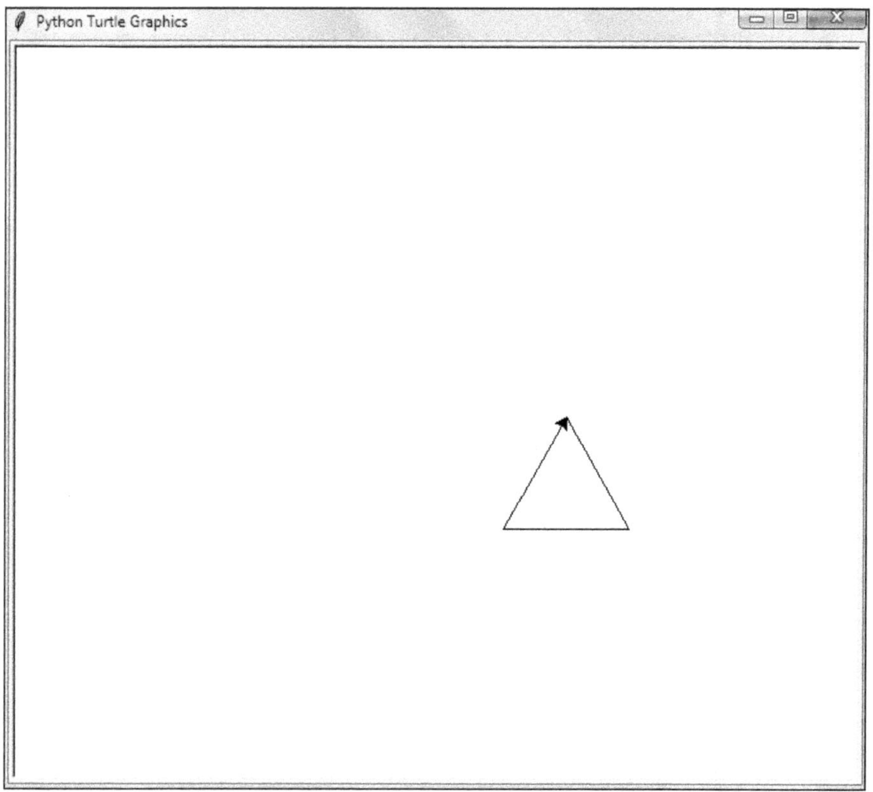

you need to do an angle caluclation to draw this shape.

*** draw a house:**

the triangle at the top should have angles that are all 60 degree

and all sides of the house should be 100 turtle steps long.the sides

of the roof will also be 100 tuetle steps long. the top left cornor of

the square where the turtle starts the output like this.

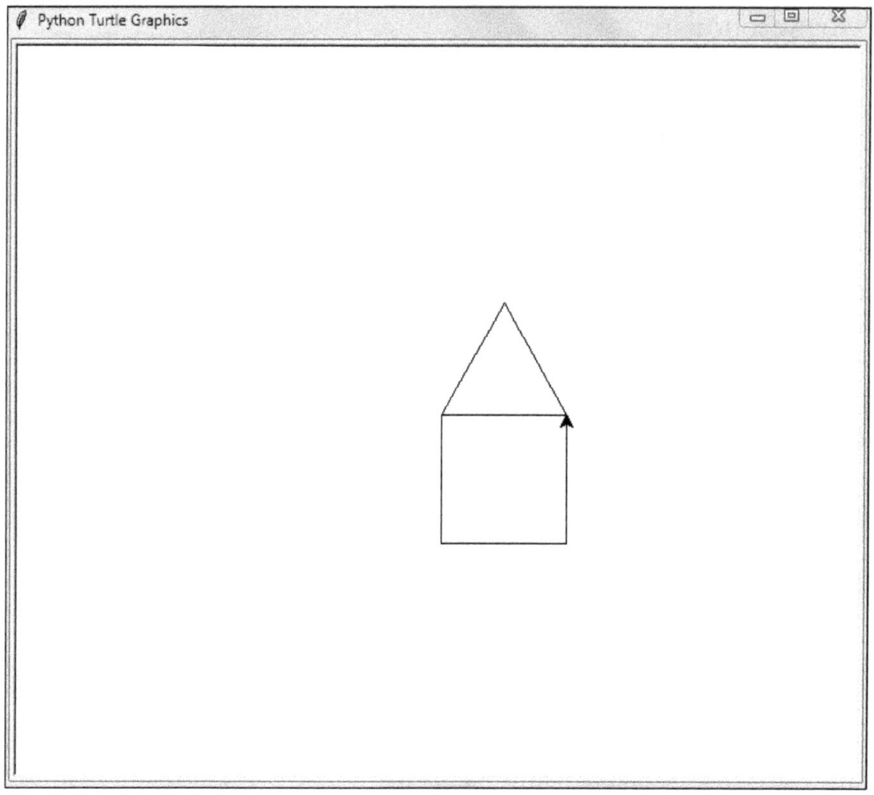

***draw a square with loop:**

write a program to draw a square with using a for loop to make

life easier! each sides should be 50 turtle steps long.

*** draw a square using loop:**

write a program to draw a square using for loop each sides should

be 50 turtle steps long.

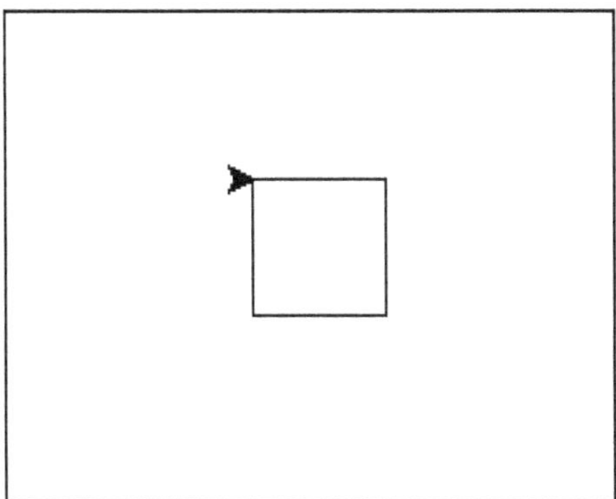

** we have already drawn one house now let`s draw a whole row of*

houses!

we have know to draw one house,and angled the turtle to the right

spot for drawing the next house. your task is to change the

program so it draw five houses in a row!

the result look like this!

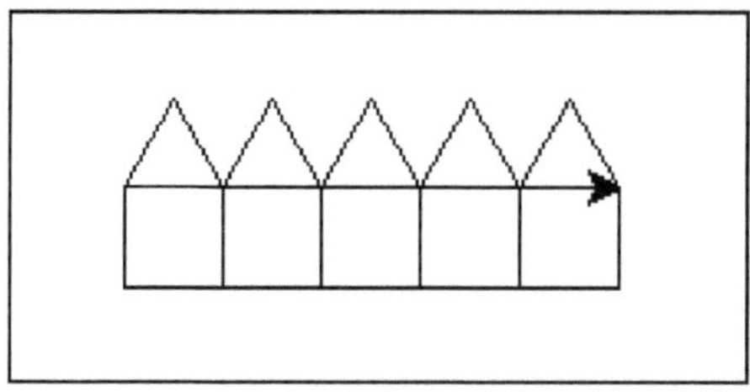

you can use for loop to sovle this problem in fast manner.

* draw a staircase:

write a program to draw a staircase of 4 steps that are 10 steps

high 30 steps wide the step will go up and to the right of the

screen as shown in the example below.

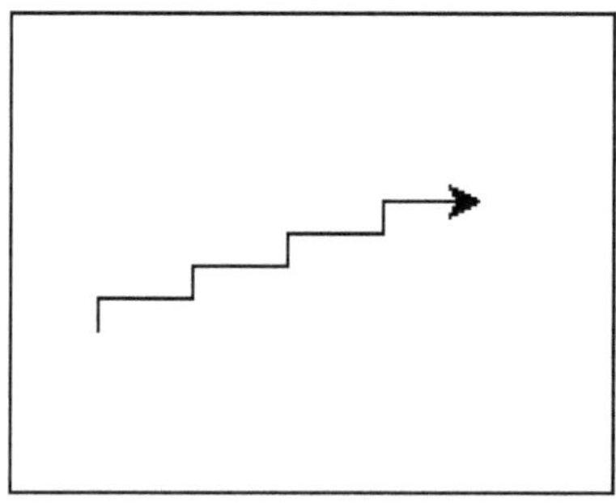

** block in a row:*

let`s draw a row of blocks!

the row should be 6 blocks long,and each square should have sides

30 turtle steps long.

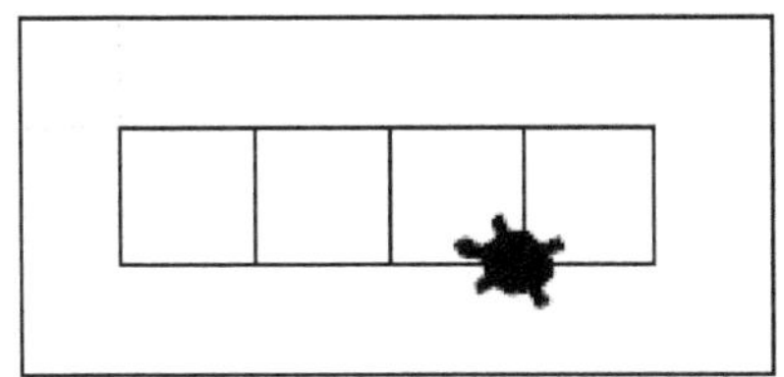

* draw square with color:

Let's add some colour to our square!

Write a program to draw a square with color i choose skyblue

color you can use your favourite color to draw a square using the turtle.

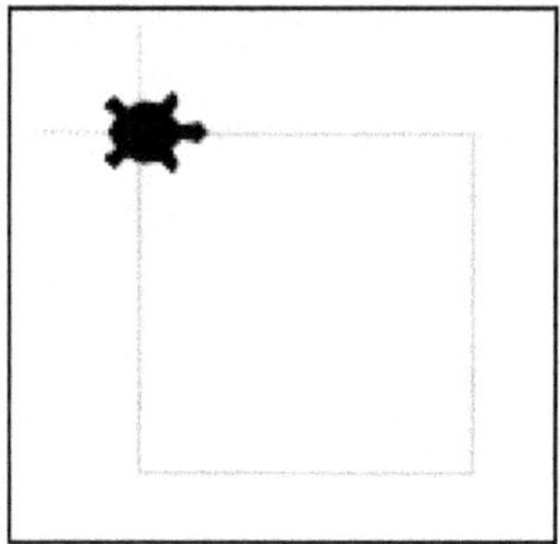

*** build a sturdy house:**

The house we draw earlier looks a bit flimsy. Let's draw one that

looks more sturdy! Draw an orange house with walls of pen size

4! Each side should be 60 turtle steps long.

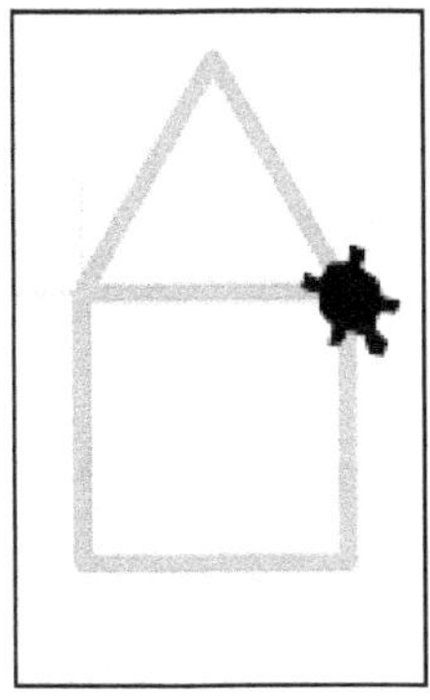

***draw a square pennant flag:**

You're going to make the turtle draw a string of 5 simple colourful

Papel picado. papel picado means mexico decorations for parties

and festivals These are very colourful squares of paper which

have beautiful cut-out designs.

You're going to make the turtle draw a string of 5 simple colourful

Papel picado.The five flags should be squares that are 20 turtle

steps long on each side, there will need to be an extra

line to join the flags together, this will also be 20 turtle steps long.

To make it super colourful you need to get the turtle to fill with

pink.

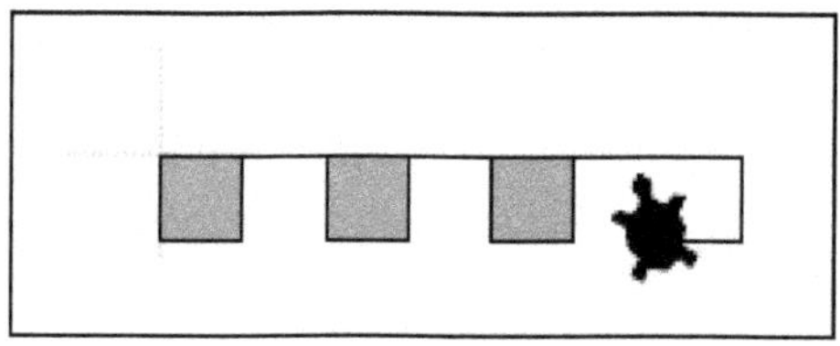

***draw a swim between the flag!**

In Australia it's very important when we go to the beach to swim

between the flags. The flags are a very specific colour pattern to make them easy to recognise. They have a red rectangle on the top

and a golden yellow colour on the bottom.

Get the turtle to draw a lifesaving flag. It should have one

rectangle on the top that is red and one rectangle on the boom

that is yellow. The rectangles should be 120 turtle steps long and

45 turtle steps high. The turtle should start on the left in the

middle of the flag.

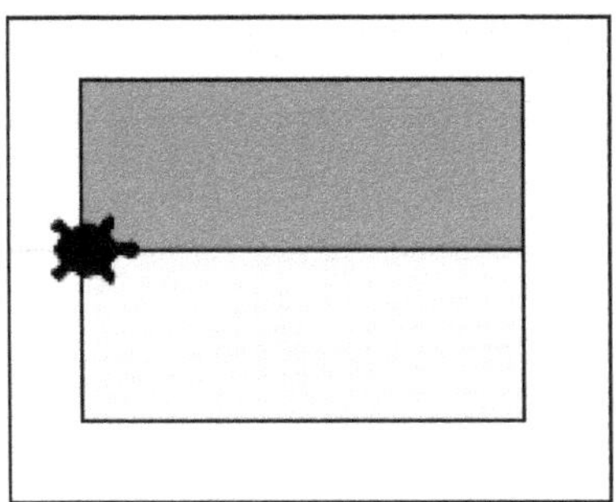

*fallout shelter:

The symbol for a fallout shelter is three black triangles on a yellow

background. Let's draw this symbol with the turtle!

Set the pencolor to dimgrey so the edges stand out.

Each side of each triangle is 100 turtle steps long and the triangles

have all angles of 60 degrees. The angle between each triangle is

also 60 degrees. The output of your program should look like this:

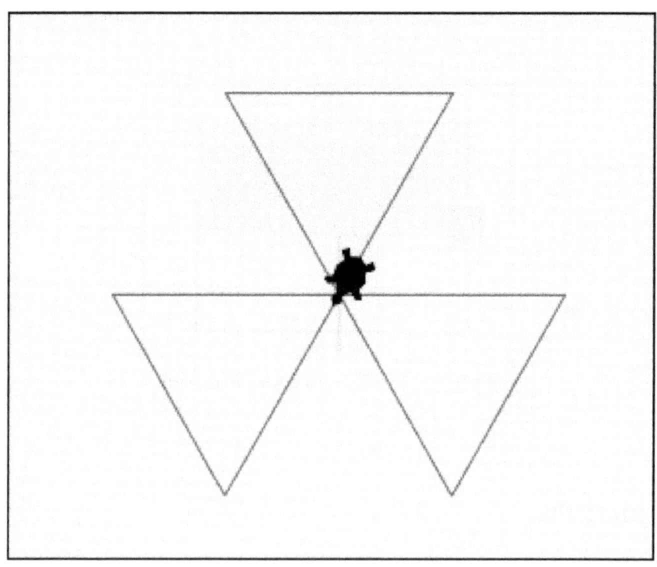

the centre of the symbol where the turtle start.

coloured cards:

In many sports, coloured cards are used to let players know if a

penalty has been awarded. For example,

yellow cards are oen a warning, and red cards send a player off.

Write a program which asks the user what colour card should be

displayed, and draws it. The card should be 80 Turtle steps wide,

and 120 Turtle steps tall. We'll only test your program using valid

colours.

The bottom lecorner should be in the center of the page, where

the turtle starts.

*step up:

Write a program that draws steps. How many steps? That's the

question! Your program should ask the user how many steps to

draw, and then draw them. Each step should be 10

Turtle steps tall, and 20 Turtle steps wide.

The steps will go up and to the right of the screen, as shown in the

example below.

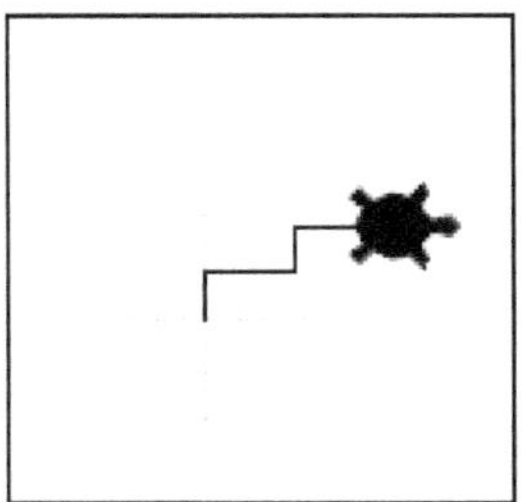

*studybot -highlighter or pen

You're building a virtual robot to help you study. You've got it

reading books, - now for highlighng and underlining notes!

Write a program that asks the user use highlighter? and either

highlights or underlines for 100 Turtle steps. If the user types in yes, you should make the pen yellow", and pen thickness 15.

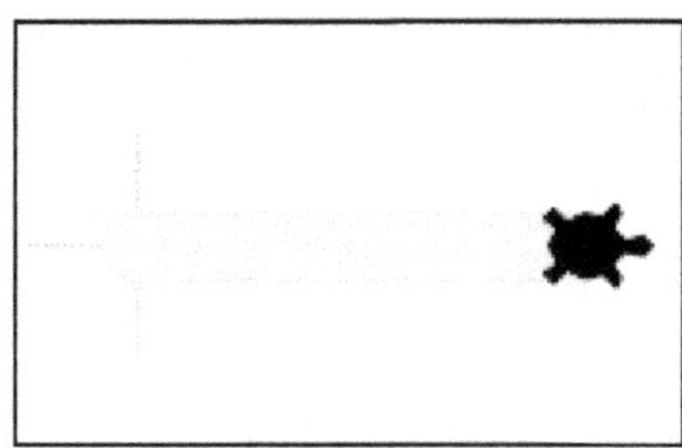

Otherwise, no matter what the user types in, you should draw a

black line 100 Turtle steps long.

Here's how the program should work if the user types in

no.

*traffic light:

You're designing a traffic light system for robots! It's a square that

is 60 Turtle steps on each side. Write a program that reads in

whether it is safe to go. If it is safe, you should draw a square with

green fil and lines of thickness 8:

If it's not safe, you should draw a red square with lines of

thickness 8:

*the three little pig:

In the fairytale The Three Little Pigs the first pig builds a house out of straw, the second sticks, and the third bricks.Write a program which asks the user whether they want to build using straw, sticks, or bricks, and then draws the house in the appropriate colour. A straw house should be orange, a stick house should be black, and a brick house should be slategray.

Material Colour

straw orange

sticks black

bricks slategray

The triangle at the top should have angles that are all 60°.

The triangle and square sides should all be 100 turtle

steps long and the pensize should be 10 for thick walls.

Here's a straw house.

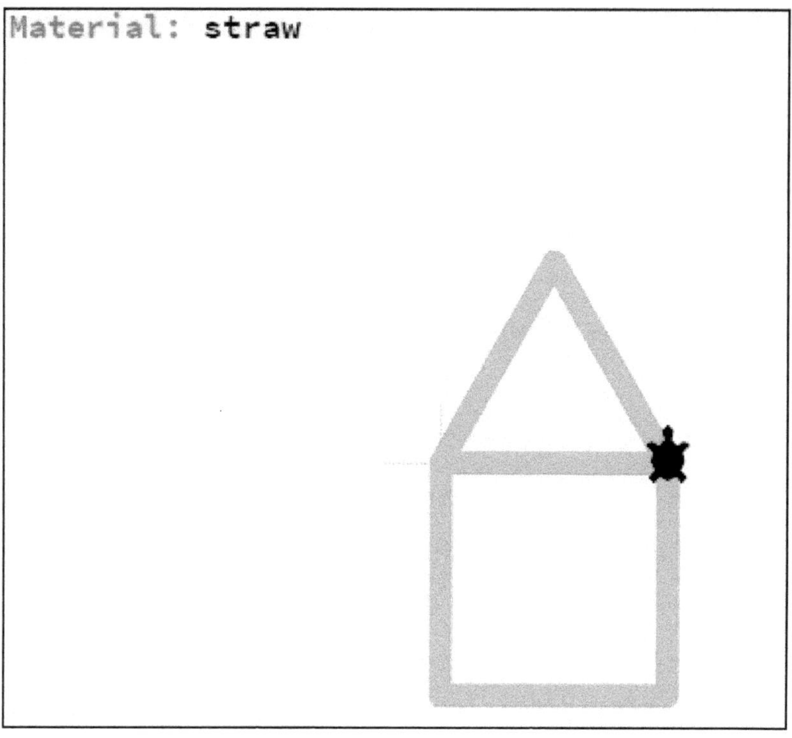

here`s stick house:

here`s brick house:

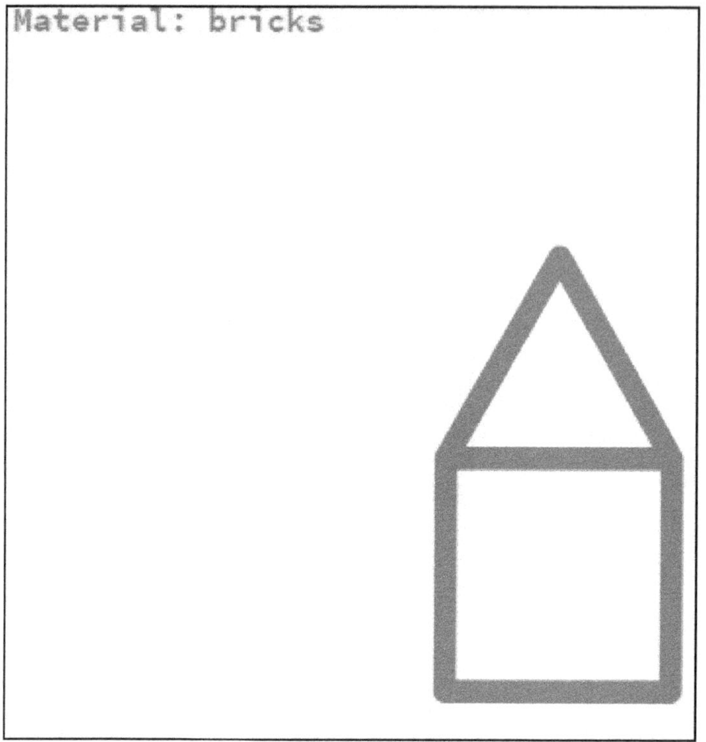

***let`s draw our heartbeat:**

If you've ever seen a movie where someone is in a hospital bed, you would have seen their heartbeat appear as a line on a heart monitor.

When a heartbeat is even, it repeats the same pattern

over and over again like this

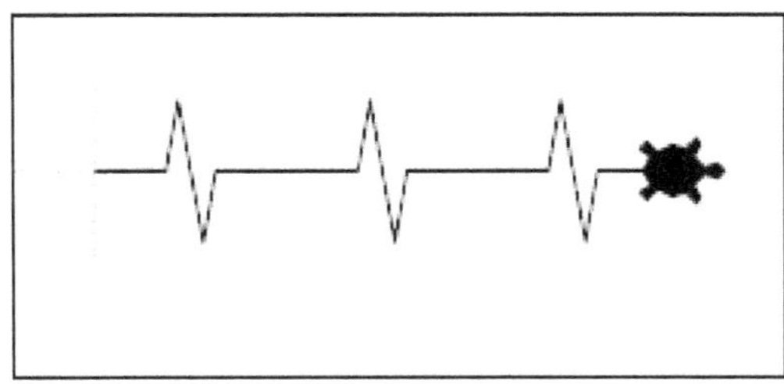

Create a heartbeat paern of 3 pulses that:

Moves 20 steps forward before the start of the pulse;

Turns 80° left draw the start of the pulse;

Moves 20 steps up to draw the start of the pulse;

Turns 160° right at the top of the pulse;

Moves 40 steps to draw the main part of the pulse;

Turns 160° leat the bottom of the pulse;

Moves another 20 steps to draw the last part of the pulse;

Has a gap of 40 steps between each pulse (the hint will help with this).

hint:

For this to work your turtle will need to face the same direction at the start and end of the loop, and the first and last thing it does is move forward 20 steps.

*draw a wooden fence:

To build the whole fence it will take 40 planks of wood, but you don't have that many.Write a program to see how much fence you can build with the planks that you have.

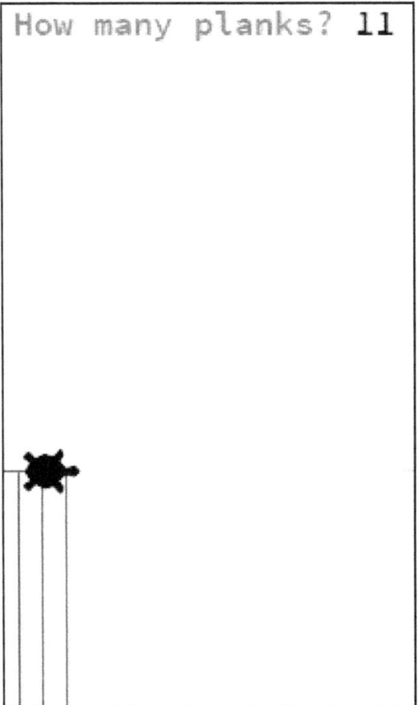

Your program should start off by moving 200 turtle steps to the left that it starts off at the left-edge of the screen. Your program should work for any number up to 40 planks. Important things to note:

**All lines should use pen colour 'brown'*

Each plank should be 100 steps high and 10 steps wide.

The top of the fence should be the center of the space.

here`s another example

draw scaleable house for ants and gaints:Let’s draw a house for ants, or for giants! We can take any shape and scale it up by mulplying all of the sides by the same number.We'll use this transformaon to draw a house of any size! Write a program which asks the user what size the house floor is (in turtle steps), the scale they want the house to be transformed by, and then uses the turtle to draw the house. The triangle at the top should have angles that are all 60° and all sides of the house should be the same number of turtle steps. Here's an example of a 50 turtle step house, scaled by 2 (so the sides all end up 50 × 2 = 100 steps long).

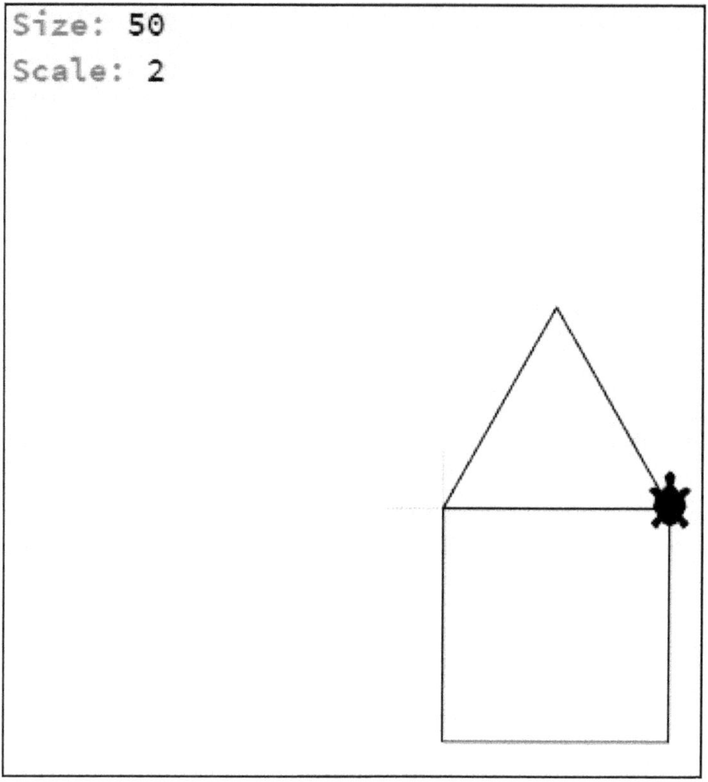

The top left of the square is where the turtle starts.

Here's another example of a much smaller house.

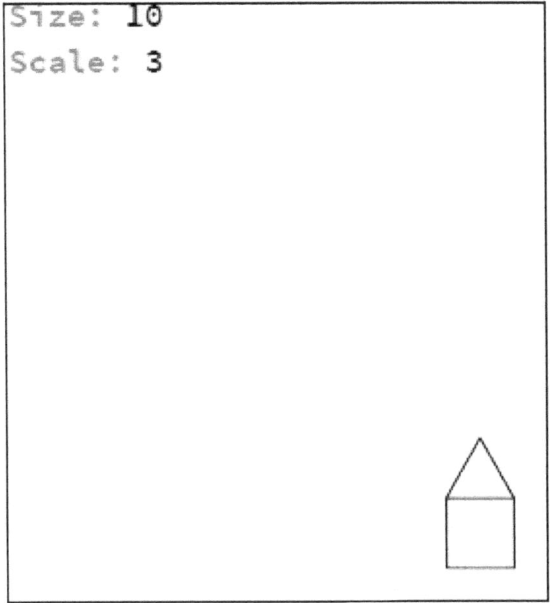

let`s draw your own playground:

Why not have a go at creating your very own drawing!

You can write whatever code you like in this question.

Consider it your personal playground.